# Parenting

## IN THE

# PEW

Guiding Your Children into the Joy of Worship

## Robbie Castleman

Foreword by
RUTH BELL GRAHAM

INTERVARSITY PRESS
DOWNERS GROVE, ILLINOIS 60515

InterVarsity Press® is the book-publishing division of InterVarsity Christian Fellowship®, a student movement active on campus at hundreds of universities, colleges and schools of nursing in the United States of America, and a member movement of the International Fellowship of Evangelical Students. For information about local and regional activities, write Public Relations Dept., InterVarsity Christian Fellowship, 6400 Schroeder Rd., P.O. Box 7895, Madison, WI 53707-7895.

"Ain't No Rock," by LaMarquis Jefferson, ©1987 Integrity's Praise Music. All rights reserved. International copyright secured. Used by permission.

"Turn Your Eyes upon Jesus" by Helen H. Lemmel, copyright ©1922 Singspiration Music/ ASCAP. All rights reserved. Used by permission of Benson Music Group, Inc.

All Scripture quotations, unless otherwise indicated, are from the HOLY BIBLE, NEW INTERNATIONAL VERSION®. NIV®. Copyright ©1973, 1978, 1984 by International Bible Society. Used by permission of Zondervan Publishing House. All rights reserved.

Cover illustration: Tim Nyberg

ISBN 0-8308-1627-5

Printed in the United States of America ∞

**Library of Congress Cataloging-in-Publication Data**

Castleman, Robbie, 1949-
    Parenting in the pew: guiding your children into the joy of worship/ Robbie Castleman.
      p.   cm.
    ISBN 0-8308-1627-5
    1. Children in public worship.   2. Worship (Religious education)
   3. Parenting—Religious aspects—Christianity.   I. Title.
    BV26.2.C37   1993
    249—dc20                          92-40659
                                            CIP

| 17 | 16 | 15 | 14 | 13 | 12 | 11 | 10 | 9 | 8 | 7 | 6 | 5 | 4 | 3 | 2 | |
|----|----|----|----|----|----|----|----|---|---|---|---|---|---|---|---|---|
| 07 | 06 | 05 | 04 | 03 | 02 | 01 | 00 | 99 | 98 | 97 | 96 | 95 | 94 | 93 | | |

For
Carolyn Park

## Foreword

This is a practical, delightful book, full of innovative ideas coupled with sound theology and spiced with irrepressible humor.

I only wish I'd had it when our children were small. Still, reading it as a great-grandmother has done me good.

By the way, Robbie's mother-in-law came to China years ago. Three missionary families hired her to teach their children. Lucy Fletcher had a profound impact on me just as I was beginning my spiritual pilgrimage. And that influence has been with me all through my life.

Enjoy this book, as I have, and you will be a better parent and a more committed Christian (without realizing it). You will be won over by Robbie's style, spontaneous humor and wise counsel.

*Ruth Bell Graham*
*Montreat, North Carolina*

## Thank You

It has been an exercise in gratitude to put on paper how good God has been to me as a parent in the pew. The living and now the writing of this book have taken nearly half of my life. My life has been and is a life inundated by the grace of God. I can trace his goodness in those he has sent to love me and encourage me along the way.

I am very thankful for my parents and sister, who have come alongside me to share the life of faith in Christ. I give thanks for Jennings and Marjorie Lee, who first opened the door to the church for our family. Unknown even to them, the hope and healing of our family began at that time.

My friend and mentor as a pastor's wife, Betty Henderson, told me "not to judge October apples in June" and modeled for me a patience in motherhood I needed to see. Clara Kendrick prays for me as I write and encourages me to be faithful.

Andy Le Peau at InterVarsity Press heard my passion for worship through a very rough draft and first suggested that I write for parents. I am grateful for his insight and for the expertise Rodney Clapp has shared to finish what was started.

And, of course, my husband, Breck, and sons Robert and

Scott are due my fondest expressions of gratitude. Breck is my pastor and dearest friend. I could sit in any pew if he was in the pulpit. Rob and Scott are my friends as well as my children. Our story is a gift of God's goodness to us as we learned to worship side by side.

And special thanks to our Carolyn Park church family. *Parenting in the Pew* was first written in your pews, first "read" by your eyes. Thank you for loving Robert and Scott. Thank you for loving Mom and Dad, too.

# Daddy, I'd Like
# You to Meet
# My Children

# 1

I wish I'd paid more attention to the significant moments
of my life. I don't remember what my husband was wearing when I met him. I do remember where and when it
happened, but I don't remember anything he said. What were
his first words to me?

Of course I didn't know that humid evening in New Orleans
would change the course of my life. I was in that city to see the
French Quarter, not to fall in love. I was distracted by the
excitement, the noise, the glitter and the yummy aromas of the
Crescent City. I should have paid attention to that interesting
young man, but I didn't.

I don't remember the first time my dad saw his first grand-child, my son Robert. Mom flew out two weeks after Robert was born, but it was five months later before Daddy ever saw or held his grandson. I don't remember how it happened because we were in the middle of a family wedding. The hubbub of dresses, flowers, shopping sprees, food, rehearsals and the reception grabbed all my attention. There were really important parts of that visit home that were lost to me.

All of us find it easy to miss the truly important moments of life. Distraction, busyness and the clamor of worry about future things rob us of what God may be up to in the present moment of our lives. We usually see the significant minutes, the turning points of our lives, from a distance. Then we pause in wonder and mutter, "Ahh, little did I realize how important that was at the time."

The lives of children are affected by moments that hardly get our attention. Given an adult's confidence and familiarity with the world, it is easy to overlook the often poignant perspective of children.

Just a few months after the *Challenger* explosion, I recall taking my boys and some of their friends to an air show. The brother of one of these friends was a five-year-old named Brandon.

The parking lot was quite a distance from the show area, so buses were provided for transportation. I casually commented, "We'll take the shuttle over from the parking lot, boys, so stay together." A few minutes later I looked over at Brandon, who had suddenly stopped his nearly ceaseless chatter. He was pale, his eyes were blinking back tears, and his chest was silently heaving with anxiety.

"Brandon, what's wrong?" I asked with concern. He shrugged his shoulders and stared straight ahead. I asked again as his tears began to fall. Suddenly it came to me—it was the "shuttle"! "Oh, Brandon," I said, "do you understand that our 'shuttle' is a bus just like you ride to school? We're not going up in the air. We are not going in a space shuttle!"

Brandon sighed in relief, and the color returned to his cheeks. His eyes sparkled with the joy of reprieve. Never was a five-year-old more grateful to climb aboard a shuttle *bus!* I had paid attention, and I was surely glad I had.

## Paying Attention Pays Off

Paying attention is not always easy for even the most well-intentioned parents. Sometimes I just want to unplug the chatterbox! I remember one time making this statement to my toddlers. The chatterbox one calmly proceeded to inform me that he couldn't be unplugged because he had batteries!

It is especially hard to pay attention to children when there is something else to pay attention to. Being immersed in a favorite TV show, an important phone call or a good book in a quiet corner seems to be a signal for your children, who suddenly find that they need your attention. The minute you settle on the couch to relax with a magazine, a teenager who hasn't spoken since last week will suddenly want to tell you all about gym class. And isn't it a wonder how the baby always needs to nurse just as Mom sits down to dinner?

Worship can be one of the times when we parents would like to pay attention to something other than our children. Kids can be distracting, aggravating and embarrassing in church. Parenthood can make sitting in a pew a lot of work. Paying attention to our children can make us less attentive to the service.

The temptations to just stay home, or at least to keep the kids out of the sanctuary, are real. It's hard to pay attention to God and children at the same time.

Training children to pay attention to God, however, is one rare way to have your cake and eat it too. Parenting in the pew can help children and parents to pay attention to what is really important.

Learning to pay attention to my children has helped me pay attention to my heavenly Father in worship. And I do remember times when my children were first held in the Father's arms. I can still see Scott's tears offered in repentance as he confessed his "grubby heart" to Jesus. I can still hear "Jesus Christ, the Crucified" boomed loudly and off-key from my toddler sons when they learned this refrain from an old hymn.

I was with them when they first understood a gospel illustration. I answered their questions about a five-syllable word used in a sermon. I was next to Robert and Scott the first time they held the sacred symbols of Christ's body and blood in their hands. I paid attention. These moments of grace and worship are remembered. And treasured.

Training your children to worship is one way to pay attention to the truly important and life-changing moments of life. Parenting in the pew keeps you focused on the significance of the moment, so it is not lost in the distractions of the day.

Training children to worship can attract parents as well as children to pay attention to what God is doing. Parenting in the pew helps you pay attention to the most important thing you can ever train your child to do: worship. Worship is the only thing we get to do forever.

For many parents, sixty minutes in a pew with a squirmy toddler or a sulky teen can seem like forever! Worship can be the farthest thing from our minds when children are distracting.

Actually, training children to worship is hard for some of us because we ourselves did not have the experience of worshiping as children. Maybe your memories of church in childhood are similar to mine.

### Petticoats and Passing Notes

I went to church as a youngster, usually in shiny shoes and an itchy petticoat. I was fairly good and reasonably quiet—at least my body was. Mentally and emotionally I romped outside, counted bricks and made up wild stories about the people in front of me. Eventually, though, I grew tired of counting bricks and doodling in the bulletin and graduated to the "teen balcony" to pass notes and gossip about the people down below.

I was a Sunday-morning dropout in my late teens, contributing to a documented trend noted in church-attendance studies. One reason for quitting was that I had never been trained to worship. I had only been told to be quiet in church.

During my childhood, my dear parents did not know the difference. Mama and Daddy did the best they could with what they knew. Mama grew up "going to church," but not to worship, while Daddy had not gone to church for any reason as a youngster.

During the early years of my childhood, my parents grieved deeply over the loss of their first child, a brother I have never known, to "crib death" (sudden infant death syndrome). Then, when I was four, we were involved in a car accident. Some people who were kind and helpful at the scene of the accident became our friends, and it was they who encouraged my parents to begin attending church and Sunday school. My mother looks back now and muses, "We knew we needed something in our lives." So we went.

As I sat by them, the difference between "going to church" and "going to worship" was something they were just beginning to discover. All I was taught was to "be quiet and be good."

"Be still, and know that I am God" is more biblical (Psalm 46:10). This verse begins to define the difference between "going to church" and "going to worship." Going to worship requires a life-transformation and happens out of a new heart, not an old habit. Going to church can be nothing more than smart time management with good intentions. It may not have much at all to do with *worship*.

## Just Going to Church

We can just go to church because it is good for us, benefits us, puts our week right, keeps our kids off drugs, and because we like the music. We can settle for going to church because it is "good for us." Giving God attention in worship may seldom influence our thinking or touch our hearts.

On more than a few occasions (usually in a ball park or a gymnasium) I have overheard the same conversation. It goes something like this:

AMY: You know, now that the kids are bigger, we really do need to get back to church. I think it would do us some good.

CHRIS: Yeah, I don't know what we'd do without our church. It keeps the kids busy. They always have something to do.

AMY: Well, Buddy isn't much for a long service. Where do you go?

CHRIS: Oh, you'd like our church. It's got some life to it! The music is terrific. Wayne and I like the sermons. They don't go on and on.

AMY: Maybe we'll visit some Sunday. Which church is it?

CHRIS: It's Riverside Presbyterian. It's the church with the big stained-glass window and all glass on one side. On the corner of Hyde and Central.

AMY: Oh, I know the one. The daughter of one of the women in our office got married there. It was real nice.

CHRIS: I like it. Now that the kids are old enough to sit with their friends, I can just sit back and relax some.

AMY: Well, that's why we waited to get back to church. It was just too much hassle when the kids were little, but I think it will do them some good now that they are older.

Why do we go to church? My parents took me because none of us were killed in a car wreck when I was four years old. They had made a promise to God.

Some people go because they promised parents or grandparents. Some people, politicians included, go because it's good for image or business. But I think most folks are like Amy and Chris and the oatmeal commercial, "It's the right thing to do."

And it is. *Worship,* however, is the rightest of reasons. But worship doesn't come naturally for us humans. God had to train the nation of Israel to worship. He went to great lengths to teach his people how he deserved to be honored and loved and known.

God outlined general guidelines ("Be still . . .") and specific rules ("With a ram prepare a grain offering of two-tenths of an ephah of fine flour mixed with a third . . ."—Numbers 15:6) for his worship. Thus God began with Israel to train a people how to worship him "in spirit and truth" (John 4:24).

God desires our worship. He commands it. His Word trains us in how to love him, how to worship him. The children of Israel, we and our children must be trained to worship.

### Wanted: Training for Worship

Parents teach their children how to make beds, hit baseballs, figure fractions and shop wisely. There are shelves of books, columns of advice and lots of good reasons for developing those skills.

But though we have plenty of advice for finances and child-rearing, very little has been written about training children to worship. In *Dr. Dobson Answers Your Questions,* James Dobson affirms that "spiritual training" is important, and he says that the first seven years of a child's life are "prime time" for this training. He provides a twenty-eight-point checklist of questions for parents.

The two checklist questions concerning church/worship are as follows:

□ Is he learning to behave properly in church—God's house?
□ Is he learning to keep the sabbath day holy?

These are two good questions. Parents need help as they try to teach their children about church. But the help they give must train children to worship, not just lessen the stress of an hour in the pew.

*Parenting in the Pew* is written to help parents train children in the only "proper behavior" for church: worship! This book is an expression of my joy in learning with my children how to remember the sabbath and keep it holy.

Parenting in the pew can be a hot battle or a holy triumph

of grace. It can consist of whispered commands: "be quiet," "shhhhh," "sit still," or it can contain the most intimate moments of life with God's family together in his presence. Sunday morning with children in the pew can be the longest hour of the week, or it can provide the very best preparation for eternal joy.

Teaching your children to worship, parenting in the pew, is entering the house of your heavenly Father and saying, "Daddy, I would like you to meet my children." Worship is seeing your Father's smile.

# Worship
# B.C.
# and A.D.

# 2

There is a big difference between worship B.C. and worship A.D.—worship "before children" and worship "after diapers"! I have heard more than a few parents confess, "I used to get more out of church before I had kids."

But the bigger issue is, What does God get out of worship? Worship is good for God. Worship concerns itself with his pleasure, his benefit, his good. Worship is the exercise of our souls in blessing God. In the Psalms we read or sing, "Bless the Lord, O my soul!" However, our chief concern is usually "Bless my soul, O Lord!"

Encountering the Lord. Meeting Jesus. Hearing his voice. Knowing God. These expectations of worship are met in hearts that are intent on his blessing. But the Lord's benefit is too seldom the thirst of our hearts, the work of our souls, the focus of our attention.

We sing "Breathe on me, breath of God," but what would we do if he did? We pray, "Come, Holy Spirit," but don't prepare for his visitation. We harmonize beautifully "Spirit of the living God, fall afresh on me," but never expect anything new. "When we've been there ten thousand years" can seem like anything but "amazing grace" if we just go to church rather than to worship. And this holds true "B.C." *or* "A.D."

Children can infringe on our worship experience. I know more than a few parents who have resented the distractions ushered into the pew by the presence of their children. Many just give up. However, children do not have to interfere with *God's* experience of worship! Worship is first a blessing to God, and he values the presence and praise of children (Matthew 18:14; Mark 10:14; Luke 18:16).

### The Meaning of Worship

Worship is not a refueling to get us through another week. Worship is not a system of traditions built up over many years of congregational life until everyone feels comfortable. Worship is not a time to unwind, relax, tune out or take a mental vacation.

Worship is not an hour of Christian entertainment. It is not what makes us good people, faithful Christians or successful parents.

Worship is the surrender of our souls to a God who is jealous for our attention, time and love. Worship is a challenge. With children it is a bigger challenge.

It has been said that modern people
□ worship their work
□ work at their play
□ and play at their worship.

We need to work at our worship. With children, we often have to work harder.

Baseball and ballet are taught through participation, practice and patience. Children learn best by doing. Great baseball players are not made in the bleachers. Dancing is not learned by remote control. Children learn to worship by worshiping— through participation, practice and patience.

The task can be overwhelming if you take it seriously. Training children to worship is a zenith of sacred trust. Unlike baseball or ballet, however, worship is best taught by parents, not "professionals."

Worship, ballet and baseball are all learned by example as well. A good trainer/teacher can hit the ball or demonstrate a pirouette. And parents in the pew can show by example what it means to seek God, to love his Son and to respond to the Holy Spirit in worship. Children learn that prayer is important when they see their parents make it a priority. Children learn to give generously when their parents do. Children dress, sing, participate by following example as well as instruction. When worship is an obvious joy to parents, children will expect to experience the same.

And the trainer can even be a single parent in the pew. On Sunday mornings, this is just what I am! My husband is the pastor, so he works every Sunday and can't sit with us. Believe me, with two boys only seventeen months apart in age, I would have appreciated two extra hands at times.

In the pew, I was the worship-trainer for our family. And Robert and Scott, now both in high school, seem to think that I did just fine. Their memories, both successes and failures, are in this book. Step by step we learned how to participate. We practiced. And practiced. And practiced. I have learned to be patient in times of discouragement, spiritual dryness and distraction. I just kept at it. I haven't always done things the way I wanted to. In the early years, training my children to worship was lonely. I didn't know anyone else who was doing the things I was doing with my boys. I wondered at times whether the effort would really make a difference.

And then a few parents began to notice the difference training was making in the pew. My friends asked me, "What are you doing? How do you do it? Why do you do it?" It got easier when these friends began to train their children too. I was encouraged to see the difference that others saw in Rob and Scott. I began to realize that the boys were learning to worship a God they loved.

I made worship training important because I wanted my sons to know God and love him. I didn't want to raise hypocrites, but holy men. I wanted my sons to love the church the way their father does. I wanted their journey of faith to be less frustrating than mine.

## A Question of Motivation

I'll tell you my story so that you can understand my motivation for worship. Sharing my struggle may encourage your own efforts to train your children to worship. If you don't have a deep motivation, an unshakable reason, for training your children to worship, participation will be hollow, practice will be inconsistent and patience will be nonexistent.

I wasn't always patient. I hated pews. I hated being told when to stand up and sit down, when to bow my head. I hated church bulletins. After all, why did anybody need one? It was the same order week after week after week after week. I hated routine and ritual. I hated "church"!

But there I was—sitting on a hard pew with a redundant bulletin, ready to stand up when signaled. Why? I had married the pastor!

Actually, my husband was just about the only thing I didn't hate that first year in the hot, humid, flat South. I was a mountain girl, used to snow skiing and sweaters. What was I doing six feet below sea level in New Orleans, sweating in a sundress?

I didn't belong to this by-the-bulletin bunch. I had come to Jesus in the late sixties, during my junior year in college. I was thrilled with the new way of life God had given me. For two years I had celebrated my new faith sitting on the grass in a park, singing freely, worshiping spontaneously and growing deeply in the rich soil of Scripture. What was I doing married to a Presbyterian minister who actually wore a suit and tie— and only brown, black or dark blue socks?

"Unfettered spontaneity" had been the characteristic of my faith that had endeared me to my husband, but I felt as if I were being robbed of my ability to worship God. After one particularly by-the-bulletin Sunday, I was tearful, homesick and ready to scream in frustration. I decided I needed some sympathy. I need to talk to someone who understood me and knew of my former style of worship and way of life.

So I called my friend Jene in California. I just knew she

would verbally pat me on the back and say, "There, there, isn't it just awful the way those Presbyterians do things?" Jene had been my Bible teacher and had always helped me see the truth. She would understand.

She did. "There is no external circumstance that can keep you from worship," she said. With greater wisdom than sympathy, Jene made her point. *I* was the problem in the pew. Jene reminded me that if the followers of Jesus could worship in chains, in hiding, in sickness, in jungles (without air conditioning), in prison or in peril, I could learn to worship in a pew with my shoes on!

Gradually I learned important lessons about worship. When I struggled in church, it was not the place or the pew that was the source of my distress. A bulletin was not the reason for the dryness of my soul. I had been spiritually thirsty because I had not understood the purpose of worship.

Worship was for God's glory, not my benefit! Although it was a good lesson, it was not an easy one to learn. I had to ask myself, did I truly love God just for himself?

I began to learn that I didn't love God as he deserved. I did love what he had done for me. I loved God so I could feel better. I had loved God easily when the snow sparkled on the ski trail, when jeans-clad, barefooted friends threw away their dope to follow Jesus and when the believers around me were just like me. I had to admit that I loved God when he satisfied my desires.

The question became, Could I meet God's desire for worship? The answer did not come quickly. It came in a Sunday-after-Sunday process. I had to practice. I had to rethink and retrain and repent. But I began to discover God's desire for worship the very next Sunday after Jene's loving rebuke. That Sunday I did not go to church; I went to *worship*. And week after week thereafter I worked to make the service a part of my heart's offering to God.

Since then I have learned that worship begins in the heart of the believer, with or without a bulletin. With or without shoes. With or without music that suits my taste. With or without stained glass, pews or grass. And with or without children! For eventually I learned, too, that I could worship with children and teach them to worship with me.

## The Challenge of Worship

The challenge of worship is to sense yourself more fully in God's presence, to sit at the feet of Jesus with the people of God, to anoint his head with the "oil of joy" (Hebrews 1:9), to bring him a "sacrifice of praise" (Hebrews 13:15). Worship means that for a time all else is set aside to be with Jesus, the Bridegroom of the church—to be together with him. To be alive in his presence!

To do this, and to give our children a sense of this passion, is to worship the Lord "in spirit and truth." A great deal of parenting in the pew is letting our children see us celebrate before the Lord. King David once taught the nation of Israel what it meant to worship: "I will celebrate before the LORD. I will become even more undignified than this, and I will be humiliated in my own eyes" (2 Samuel 6:21-22).

It is not a simple thing to be humiliated in your own eyes and to be before the Lord alone. A toddler can certainly contribute to the humble part, but make it very difficult to concentrate on being with the Lord. But if our hearts are fixed on being with our children before the *Lord* and not before the congregation, we will begin to experience great relief and freedom.

We can be freed to help our children worship without the pull of external distractions or the self-consciousness of wondering what others are thinking. We can overcome the question that bothers so many parents with children in the pew: What do people think of *me* because of the way my children behave?

*Joy* is the last word many parents would choose to describe what it's like to sit in a pew with their children. Resentment and frustration are not uncommon feelings for people who "before we had kids" experienced an hour of peace and calm in the pew. Parenting in the pew can be a hassle. Or it can be holy. It depends on who we are and how we see ourselves. Do we sit with our children "in church" or "in worship"?

Too many adults who learned how to be quiet in church are still doing just that. And many of them are passing this along to their children. A family can learn to sit still very well, but be unmoved by the holy presence of God.

God invites families to "be still and know" him. Jesus desires the praise and worship of children. He delights in the songs of infants. God calls us to worship him; he *commands* it. In fact, so serious is this to him that if we humans fail to worship, rocks may take our places.

> When [Jesus] came near the place where the road goes down the Mount of Olives, the whole crowd of disciples began joyfully to praise God in loud voices. . . . Some of the Pharisees in the crowd said to Jesus, "Teacher, rebuke your disciples!"
>
> "I tell you," he replied, "if they keep quiet, the stones will cry out." (Luke 19:37-40)

Parenting in the pew is the process of putting a few rocks out of work!

# Praise
# and
# Puppies

# 3

I n the imaginations of youngsters, doctors live in hospitals and teachers live at school. And more than a few children in our years of ministry have been surprised to see my husband at places other than the church building. I remember being in the supermarket one day when we came upon a mother and son from our congregation. The kindergartner whispered to his mom in a voice full of wonder, "Mom! Mr. Breck gets his groceries here, too!"

Children identify people with places in rather concrete ways. Sometimes ideas get mixed up with amusing results. My husband "looks like Jesus." If there is a play, Breck gets to be Jesus, because he is tall, thin and bearded, and has rather shaggy curly hair. Add to this my husband's gentle nature and deep kindness, and one can understand how a child could be confused.

One morning three-year-old Matthew waited in the pew for Breck to enter the sanctuary. But we were gone on vacation, and the visiting pastor entered instead. He was a godly man, I am sure, but he was short and balding and had no beard. Matthew was disappointed, to say the least. I wish I could have been there to see this toddler stand up on the pew, stomp his foot and ask loudly, "Well, where's Jesus?"

Matthew just expected Jesus to be at church, and the pictures in his Bible and Sunday-school papers sure looked a lot like the fellow who talked about God every week. It was a delight to hear this story and to see Breck, the very next week, take Matthew in his office for a chat. Breck's stock probably dropped some after that, but the Lord was pleased. God delights in children, in their expectancy, in their vulnerability and ability to believe.

These are gifts of grace that children bring to a church family. Parenting in the pew encourages children to participate in the life of the church, to share these gifts of unfettered faith and expectation. Children can enhance the worship of God for the whole congregation.

### Children Believe

Children are a symbol of the kingdom, indeed the "greatest" in the kingdom. Matthew records,

At that time the disciples came to Jesus and asked, "Who is the greatest in the kingdom of heaven?"

He called a little child and had him stand among them.

And he said: "I tell you the truth, unless you change and become like little children, you will never enter the kingdom of heaven. Therefore, whoever humbles himself like this child is the greatest in the kingdom of heaven. And whoever welcomes a little child like this in my name welcomes me." (Matthew 18:1-5)

We need children in our churches. They can remind us vividly what it means to be great believers. Young children have the capacity to accept as truth what is told to them by adults. Even at fairly early ages they can learn to tell the difference between the imaginary and the real if this distinction is made by trusted adults. But children delight in believing what adults find difficult to swallow. The ideas of faith we share need careful telling.

Jesus used the idea of the unseen wind to illustrate the reality of the Spirit. The adult Nicodemus in John's third chapter needed such an illustration to help him grasp the truth. Children also find stories, illustrations and word-pictures helpful for grasping ideas of faith that cannot be apprehended with the five senses.

Children are willing to believe, and this means that their hearts have a great capacity for worship. Young children desire to "see" Jesus, to love him, to be with him. More than a few parents have had to deal with questions about dying after a description of heaven as the place "where Jesus lives."

I remember our oldest urgently telling my husband to "pull over!" after one such discussion in our car. With its constant heavy traffic, Claiborne Avenue in New Orleans is no street to "pull over" on. Well, that was four-year-old Robert's point: "We could all hold hands and lay down in the street and go see Jesus together!"

This same son asked about our obvious grief over the death of a teenager in our youth group. Leukemia had claimed Tim's life about a week before Christmas. When we told Robert of Tim's death, our toddler jumped up and down with joy and envy! We asked if he had understood what we meant. Robert replied with wide-eyed wonder, "Oh, Tim is so happy! He gets to see Jesus blow out the candles on his birthday cake!"

Yes. And Jesus knew that this delightful faith and fervent love makes for kingdom All-Stars.

Chronological age is important to consider when paying attention to how children think about God and how they learn to worship. Although individual children are certainly very different, there are general similarities among children that are helpful to bear in mind.

Grade-school children have a more informed and sober approach to faith than preschoolers like Matthew, but they are seldom less willing to believe. They just want to know more.

Older grade-school children have learned that parents and teachers can be wrong, but they still don't expect them to be. Yet they will ask questions—lots of questions. Adults need to give careful and truthful answers. Scripture needs to be cited time and again as the resource for many answers.

Children tend to believe what they read. Children of this age group need to see that faith is no fairy tale. They may no longer assume that Jesus lives at church, but they need to be confident that he lived in real history.

Teenagers aren't as tough as they seem when it comes to worship. In fact, worship can help them deal with a crucial question of faith: "How do I myself know that all this is true?" Teenagers may borrow their parents' car, but they need to own their own faith. Worship can make all the difference between "borrowed" faith and "owned-for-myself" faith.

Teens want to encounter God. They want to hear God speak back to them when they pray. They want to know about the faith of others. Teens also want to do something for God. Worship needs to be a big part of that. Too often teens are told that mowing the church lawn or tending the church nursery is all they can do for God. Worship is seldom seen as "serving" God, even though the hour between eleven and noon is called the "worship service."

From toddlers to teens, kids have a substantial capacity for worship. God knows that children are quite ready to believe the truth. Parents need to ask them to listen to it in worship. We need to help them listen. And we need to listen to them when they respond to what they've heard.

## Children Respond

Participation in every syllable of the service is of major importance in training children to worship. But remember, sometimes an encounter with God won't look like one at first. God can surprise us with his presence. And children often are the leaders in boldly approaching the throne of grace.

Jeremy is a dear friend's middle son. One Sunday Jeremy sat with my two grade-school-aged sons and me. Jeremy was four. Barely. During the responsive reading Jeremy was standing on the pew. As I had learned to do with toddlers, my arms circled around him as I held the book for him to see, and I pointed to the words as the reading progressed.

My arms provided control and support. We were concentrating on every word. Even though he was too young to read,

Jeremy followed my finger as it pointed to the black words said
by the pastor and the red words recited by the congregation. We
were reflecting together on the amazing personal knowledge
God has of each one of us from Psalm 139.

You know when I sit and when I rise. . . .

My frame was not hidden from you
    when I was made in the secret place.

Jeremy listened to the words, watched my finger intently.

How precious to me are your thoughts, O God!

Suddenly Jeremy cried out in an excited whisper, "Aunt Robbie, Aunt Robbie!" (All the children in that church called me
"Aunt.") Looking into his sparkling dark brown eyes and ec-
static smile, I interrupted my own reading to whisper, "Jeremy,
what is it?"

"Aunt Robbie," Jeremy whispered back energetically, "Jesus
knows my dog!"

At first I was stumped. He repeated his discovery with great
joy. I thought about the psalm the congregation had just con-
cluded, and remembered Jeremy's dog—a fuzzy mongrel named
Precious. That was it! I suddenly saw what Jeremy had heard
and understood so well.

"How precious to me are your thoughts, O God!" Jeremy had
heard the word and made an odd connection, but hadn't missed
the point! He was right. The God we were encountering knows
our getting up and our lying down. He knows our frame and
the length and content of days lived and yet to come. This God
surely does know about Jeremy's dog, Precious!

That four-year-old was learning to worship. Jeremy responded to God with the excitement and wonder and joy that
David's psalm was intended to provoke in all of us. God knows

all about us! If you have a dog, God knows its name.

God was praised that day by Jeremy's joyous discovery. God was worshiped and adored in that bundle of energy. God was blessed because Jeremy was expected to participate in every part of the liturgy. And because he was helped to do so even as a four-year-old. And because he was *there*.

## Children Belong

In their book *Resident Aliens: Life in the Christian Colony,* Stanley Hauerwas and William Willimon affirm the wisdom of including children in the worship and work of the kingdom. Nestled almost parenthetically in their chapter on ethical conduct in the Christian community is this observation:

> In many of our modern, sophisticated congregations, children are often viewed as distractions. We tolerate children only to the extent they promise to become "adults" like us. Adult members sometimes complain that they cannot pay attention to the sermon, they cannot listen to the beautiful music, when fidgety children are beside them in the pews. "Send them away," many adults say. Create "Children's Church" so these distracting children can be removed in order that we adults can pay attention.

These professors at Duke University conclude their point by noting,

> Interestingly, Jesus put a child in the center of his disciples, "in the midst of them," in order to help them pay attention. . . . The child was a last-ditch effort by God to help the disciples pay attention to the odd nature of God's kingdom. Few acts of Jesus are more radical, countercultural, than his blessing of children. (Nashville: Abingdon, 1989, p. 96)

Now, it must be acknowledged that some churches have developed "children's church" for reasons other than sending fidgety children away for an hour. Some churches have a children's church to help prepare children for the adult service, to learn creeds and hymns and the meanings behind rituals. Many churches settle for another version of "Sunday school" with lessons and activities. Even though I consider the former more useful than the latter, I wouldn't be writing this book if I felt it was best. Churches sometimes develop programs for children because parents are not equipped or willing to train their children in the things of faith.

## Children Can Help

Parents are the best people to teach their children what it means to worship God. And I believe that parenting in the pew helps adults as well as their offspring to "pay attention." Children have wonderful ways of making a point that every preacher dreams his congregation will get! Children tend to respond immediately to an idea that grabs their attention.

Pastors of the quietest congregations know the joy of hearing an audible answer to rhetorical questions that punctuate a sermon. One time my husband gave a call to missions in the Lord's words from Isaiah 6:8: "Whom shall I send? And who will go for us?" He paused for effect and a first-grader called out, "I'll go if my mom will let me!"

More than a few parents have had to comfort their children when the suffering of Good Friday touched tender hearts. I remember the tears of my boys when they understood Jesus' sacrifice for their sin for the first time. They felt so grieved that it had to be that way. Children remind those of us more familiar

with the truths of Scripture how we should respond. They remind us all what it means to "marvel" at God's grace like those
who first received it.

Children help us to pay attention to what God is really saying. The first-grade missionary and Jeremy both displayed the
deep capacity of children to respond to God, to worship in spirit
and truth. They responded to the truth of God with awestruck
insight—with *worship*.

God was in church on those Sundays, reminding all of us that
he knows everything about us, asking us to go and love the
world for his sake. Jeremy and that first-grade missionary
whose name I cannot remember responded with eager joy. And
I'm sure that Jeremy could reassure what's-his-name that God
knows everything and would never forget his name!

# Sunday Morning
## Starts
## Saturday Night

# 4

I t's a fact: More shoes are lost on Sunday morning than all other days of the week combined. Is "Hurry up!" the Sunday-morning call to worship in your home? Does the pressure of finding shoes, scolding a slow one and settling fights over the newspaper funnies diminish your sense of sabbath rest? Does your hypocrisy quotient increase as the tension of getting out of the house gives way to a warm "Hello!" for the church people you don't live with?

Are you discouraged by the sibling squabbles in the back seat that dismantle the "neat and tidy" look within seconds? Do you habitually run out of adequate change for the Sunday-school offering? Remember you forgot to practice the memory verse with your grade-schooler? Wish your high-schooler would wear a coat and tie without a fight just once?

Do you wonder more often than you'd admit why Sunday mornings are even included in the Christian life? Why do Sunday mornings seem shorter than Saturday mornings? Why do Saturday nights tend to end later? Do you ever mentally prepare lunch during the last verse of the final hymn?

In the dictionary *worship* comes right after *worn, worn-out, worry, worrywart, worse* and *worsen.* Sometimes on Sunday mornings worship follows the same sequence. Getting children and young people to the worship place is too often as far as we get in helping our offspring to worship. As the dropout rate of older kids indicates, there has got to be a better way!

Sunday morning should be a time of joyous expectation for a family who loves the Lord. But too often it is a morning riddled with strife and filled with regret.

Recently I listened to a group of parents share their frustrations with Sunday mornings. These were parents whose lives are given to Christian ministry—parents steeped in Scripture, parents committed to rearing their children in ways that honor the Lord. Even though I understood, my heart just broke as Sunday morning was described as "the worst morning of my week." One mother confessed, "Sometimes I'm relieved to stay home if one of the kids is sick." Another shared, "I'm just exhausted by the time I get to church."

As I sat listening, I thought about my two teenage sons. Sunday mornings are some of our best memories. I know how much I miss my sons when they aren't beside me in the pew.

Now high-schoolers, Rob and Scott spend summers in short-term missions overseas. I miss their companionship in the pew at those times.

I've had some Sundays when all did not go as planned (usually for lack of planning!), and I've experienced, on occasion, the weariness my friends were expressing. But for the most part, our Sunday mornings have been times of joy and closeness, not strife and estrangement. What has made the difference?

### Working to Worship

There is a way to turn the hearts of our children to worship and take the *worry* and *worn-out* from the Sunday-morning agenda. The key lies in another, better "w" word: *work*.

The sanctuary is often described as a place to "just relax and unwind," providing a once-a-week hour of reprieve from the demands of the world. It's no wonder that this hour can also become a reprieve from God's command to worship him.

Worship is work, hard work. It is also rewarding work. To worship the Lord "in spirit and truth" does not come easily, and it certainly does not come naturally to us. It is difficult to worship on the leftover energy of a long week and a late Saturday. The Sunday-morning encounter with God is worthy of our best energy, not our least.

The Lord of life promises to accompany us in worship. We will come upon unexpected stores of energy when we remember that worship is a joyous privilege. His mighty energy will be at work in us to revitalize our weary spirits. We will find rest for our souls.

Sundays are special. Children know that there is a difference between a birthday cake and an any-day cake. Birthday cakes are planned, designed in a special way and focused on the person being celebrated. A birthday cake is the person's favorite; the frosting is sweeter, and the anticipation is so thick you could cut it with a knife! An any-day cake can be eaten without much introduction, but a birthday cake is eaten after candles and songs and ceremony.

Technically, cake is cake. It's the day, the parents and the preparation that set birthday cakes apart. Birthday cakes are cakes with an attitude!

Worship is loving the Lord with an attitude. We love the Lord every day, but Sunday is God's favorite flavor and the frosting is sweeter.

## Heart Preparation

Preparing a special cake or birthday party begins with a desire in our hearts to give honor on a special day. I know that I have a much better frame of mind on a busy celebration day if I have gone through an attitude check. I need to remember why all of this is worth doing.

Parenting in the pew begins with an attitude check. Are you eager or going through the motions? Are you profoundly grateful for the saving work of Christ on the cross, or are you religious by habit or culture? Are you more conscious of how God sees you in worship than of how others see you in church? Is worship time priority time? Do you talk about preparations for worship during the week? Do your children sense that, just as they look forward to birthdays, you can hardly wait for Sunday to get here?

Parenting in the pew, teaching our children to worship, is a sacrifice of praise and thanksgiving that God rejoices to receive.

So how do we begin the practical work of preparing this offering once our attitude is poised on tiptoes of expectancy and love? Well, Sunday morning begins on Saturday night. Our children need to hear us say to friends or baby sitters, "No, we won't be too late; we are set to worship God tomorrow morning."

## Home Preparation

Sunday mornings seem shorter than other mornings because they often start later. For many of us, it's much easier to get up early on Saturday to prepare a picnic than it is to get up early on Sunday to prepare our sacrifice of praise. The call to worship begins with the chime of the alarm clock that is set with sabbath rest in mind.

Starting with infants, who seem to require an enormous amount of baggage for every contingency, Sundays need to embrace the calm of sabbath rest. Some of the distress reflected in infant fussiness in the church nursery begins with parental hurry and stress. One way to make the Sunday nursery setting acceptable to your youngest children is to take time upon arrival to linger and share that space with the infant or pretoddler. This, in turn, is easier if plans are made and all the baby's necessities are packed up early.

With older children, beginning with toddlers, start Sundays with an announcement that the very best day of the week is about to begin. When my boys were small I set the tone by telling them, "Jesus is excited! This is his special day!"

Not only was this true, but as they got older the specialness of the day grew with them. One custom was our "Jesus music" on Sunday mornings. It is a little harder to get short-tempered when "Sing Alleluia" lingers in the air.

It is true that Sunday mornings seem more complicated than other mornings. The schedule is different, the entire family may have different responsibilities for the morning at church, and usually all members of the family leave home at the same time. In addition to this, the Christian family must recognize that we have an enemy, one who delights in hypocrisy and distraction. The devil, in all of his evil power, wants to undo the worship we prepare for God. It is no surprise that Sunday morning can be a time of spiritual warfare.

Good warriors prepare for the battle and do not encourage the advance of the enemy. God's Word warns and commands us to "remember the Sabbath day by keeping it holy." God gave us this admonition because of our constant temptation to forget God and only keep up appearances. Special efforts of grace and faith on Sunday mornings are needed to win the battle. These efforts need not be extravagant, just faithful. Sometimes putting on the "full armor of God" (Ephesians 6:10-18) begins with finding a pair of socks that match!

## Dressing for Worship

Clothes, shoes and socks for Sunday need to be readied by Saturday evening. Children need to help set the agenda for what to wear. Kids are different! One child may find it delightful to "wear a tie like Dad" or "shiny shoes like Mom" on Sundays. Another child (same parents, same rearing, same everything!) thinks a clean T-shirt without a slogan is more than enough.

One of my childhood memories of Sunday mornings was having to wear stiff dresses I couldn't breathe in, let alone drink punch, play or pray in! So I've never had much interest in investing in "Sunday clothes" for my kids or myself. I wanted them to dress for worship, not for me. My older son is Mr. Casual; he wore a tie for the basketball team before he ever wore a tie to church (and didn't like it much then!). On the other hand, my younger son enjoys dressing up and likes to "look good" all the time.

I actually believe my husband got a raise once because the church thought our son Scott had only one shirt—his favorite purple one. I think that for an entire year purple was his personal liturgical color.

I must confess that just last year what one dear son wore gave me a start. I probably wouldn't have noticed except that it was youth-collect-the-offering Sunday. Even I found it a bit distracting to see a RADICAL DUDE in neon pass the plate! After the service I drew him aside and began, "Dear, about your shirt . . ."

"Oh, Mom, I know!" he interrupted, blushing. "I shouldn't have worn this shirt today. I forgot about it being my turn to collect the offering." We laughed. I told him to tell me if any criticism came his way—I'd help him out.

The point is, I never wanted what my children wore to compete for their attention in preparing to encounter God in worship. We allowed them to dress as they liked—as long as it was ready to be worn by Saturday evening. Too many Sundays are lost with lost socks. Too many Sundays are overshadowed by what we wear and how we look.

### Thinking Ahead: A Tithe or a Tip
In addition to advance planning for what to wear, anticipating

what the family needs can help return joy to Sunday mornings. Memory verses can be rehearsed on Saturday. Supplies for Sunday-school projects can be obtained ahead of time—that is, if the children happen to remember, before you are pulling into the church parking lot, that they were supposed to bring twelve colors of felt for the twelve-tribes-of-Israel display. Remember, we can only do so much and nothing is foolproof.

Money for the offering is a constant need from Sunday to Sunday, though, and this gives parents the opportunity to teach children an important aspect Christian obedience. Teaching children to tithe can be an exciting part of learning to trust God and participate in the work of his people.

Begin at the earliest age to have children prepare their offering for Sunday. If your church uses envelopes for this purpose, it can be helpful for each child in the family to have them. Usually the envelopes are numbered and provide a place for the name of the giver. Younger children like to write their names, and this can give them a greater sense of importance and involvement in their gift.

If your church uses faith pledges for giving, children should be involved in the process as much as this is appropriate. Preschool children can commit a set amount of money. When arithmetic days begin, parents can teach the concept of tithing. Even ten percent of a two-dollar allowance is important to the Lord when it is offered in faith and obedience. These two spiritual gifts are worth far more than twenty cents.

It has been a pleasure to see Rob and Scott grow in their commitment to tithe. During grade school, they looked in their wallets each week and figured out what ten percent was and gave that. Some of this money was left over from the previous week's allowance, which had already been tithed. I wasn't about to clarify that money is usually tithed once.

As they have entered their teen years, I have become more detached from the process; they figure out their own commitment in giving. They understand that ten percent is where to begin rather than a goal one hopes to reach eventually. When Rob and Scott are short on money, it is usually because they are behind on their chores or have not been faithful in their giving. Trusting God in the area of finances is an important lesson to learn over a lifetime.

Once one of the boys wanted a pair of special tennis shoes. He knew that if he tithed, the shoes would be financially out of reach. On this occasion he gave a tithe in faith if not in joy. The next week, the shoes he wanted went on sale and he was able to buy them. As we left the shoe store he commented, "Mom, I think I got these shoes because I tithed. I almost didn't. Wow, now they are really special."

Now admittedly, anyone can begin to play manipulative games with the theology of tithing. But in this case I think God picked a lesson that would communicate to a fifteen-year-old boy. Shoes are a very big deal to a boy, and faith is a very big deal to God. Learning to put God first and trust him to provide is no small lesson for anyone.

Teaching children to tithe can help develop a generous attitude about giving praise, time, goods and blessing to God. Even very young children can be given money to place in the plate or offering envelope. It is good if children can feel that what is given away is something from themselves, not the parent. Toddlers and preschoolers are not often given a set allowance for household chores. If they are given money for the offering, then, it should be given to them with a sense of being personally under their charge and keeping. Putting the money in their own pockets or purses lends a sense of possession and special purpose. It is best if this money is given at home on Saturday night or Sunday morning, and not at the last minute.

Too many parents give their kids pocket change to put in the plate, just as they let the children push the buttons in elevators. Not only is this not an offering from the child's resources, but it communicates that God can be honored with a "tip" rather than a tithe. Many people end up tipping God with leftovers all their lives—and pretty skimpy tips at that. Ten percent is the starting point for tipping, even for mediocre service!

### Coming to Worship
Children need to sense our excitement about worshiping with God's people. Too many conversations to and from church are filled with complaints and discontent—criticisms of pastors, programs and fellow parishioners. Instead, children need to hear how the Lord met us in worship, how much we learned in Sunday school, what we love about our church family. Our children need to see through us how the Spirit is at work for his purposes in our communities of faith. A heart of gratitude and eyes of faith are easier to have when Sunday is more holy and less hassle.

I always try to keep Sunday simple. Breakfast is juice and rolls or doughnuts that we don't have other days of the week. I don't prepare a special lunch or leave anything cooking in the oven. We habitually have college students or lonely parishioners over for lunch. Most times it's hot dogs or tuna sandwiches that our guests help prepare. Working in the kitchen and helping to set the table is more like home to folks than a fancy meal that preoccupied the cook during worship. People who fuss less usually practice hospitality more!

Keeping Sunday simple can help keep Sunday special for God. The sabbath rest was given to free up our time so that we could pay attention to the Lord. We need to recapture God's intention for setting aside time for community worship as well as private daily devotion.

The Lord "looks at the heart," not at "outward appearance" as we do (1 Samuel 16:7). I may have been disconcerted by the RADICAL DUDE shirt my son wore to collect the offering, but God saw deeper things. It would have been worse for this son to forsake his responsibility to collect the offering because he felt self-conscious about his attire. The service was put above himself. Of course, it would have been even better for my "radical dude" to have remembered this responsibility Saturday night and set out something less distracting. People do look at outward appearance. Even without a critical spirit, others should not be deterred from their efforts to concentrate on the Lord in their worship.

The correct balance comes when we first consider the inward disposition of our hearts. This is what God sees. What makes my heart most ready for worship is what is important.

Simple Sundays and casual clothes help in our home. In a fairly distant second place we consider the outward appearance that can affect our community. Once people know your heart, however, this is less important; they won't really care what you wear or what you feed them for lunch. Folks really love my "radical dude." And no one said a word of complaint about his T-shirt.

## Called to Worship

The call to worship centers on the One who calls us. This call is not a friendly suggestion, but a loving command. God is worthy of our worship. He alone is a worthy recipient of our adoration and praise. He is watchful when we worship.

God sees us. He sees our posture, our faces, our antics in the pew. He knows our hearts and minds. One of the first things I began to impress upon my children was this fact: God is present. He is looking at you, and he cares about how you show him that you love him, that you think he is special.

God sees me. So do my children. I let my kids watch me prepare for worship, sense my anticipation, get ready for God's favorite day. And I have tried to make Sunday morning our favorite time of the week. With few hassles and regrets, our Sundays have become a holy joy. We know that God loves radical worship from dudes and their parents!

# Counting Bricks
# or Encountering
# God

# 5

Ask any nine-year-old who goes to church and she can tell you
□ how many beams cross the church ceiling
□ how many bricks there are between the floor and ceiling of the sanctuary
□ how many red pieces there are in any stained-glass window
□ how many people in the choir have gray hair or glasses, or don't pray with their eyes shut

Now of course this all depends on the sanctuary structure, but regardless of whether the building is Gothic or gymnasium, kids have counted all sorts of stuff to keep them occupied during worship.

Why is it that children who refuse to nap all week nod off before the preacher is three sentences into the sermon? Any child can tell you that it takes a lot of energy to "sit still and be quiet" during church. Most children will testify, too, that coloring in all the *o*'s in the bulletin is harder than it seems. Especially with all the interruptions for hymns, creeds and offerings.

One of the biggest challenges for parenting in the pew is training children to pay attention to what is happening—the worship of God—and making them a part of it.

Ask adults what they remember about church as a child, and the responses will most often mention the music, the building itself or how hard it was to sit still. A lot of us counted bricks, colored in the *o*'s and daydreamed, or really dreamed, during the sermon.

Adults who do recall some spiritual impact usually connect them to services or occasions that were unusual—perhaps a funeral, or a revival with a guest speaker, or a special service of music. These types of services can make long-lasting impressions on children.

When something in worship is different or unusual, it holds a child's attention longer. This is true for most things in our children's culture. Entertainment has become a standard part of American expectations for education. The creativity of "Sesame Street" and other early-learning programs popularized the idea that we entertain to teach. The generation of young people who learned their ABC's with Big Bird demanded video with their music as they grew into adolescent years. Music videos and

MTV grew out of this generational TV experience.

The idea that successful worship is entertaining is not considered outlandish in our culture. "Sesame Street" saints want to be entertained. They expect creativity to hold their attention. Entertainment can be furnished by the service itself or by well-meaning parents who provide coloring books or games to "entertain" children and keep them quiet during church.

But worship-as-entertainment will not accelerate the spiritual growth of our children. (Educational entertainment has not improved our children's scholastic abilities either!) Worship needs to be the one realm in our culture that refuses to accept the world's addiction to be entertained in order to learn.

This does not preclude creativity or change in worship, but it does mandate that worship liturgies be designed for God's pleasure and not our entertainment. At the same time, God's desire does address a child's recognition of spiritual needs and interest.

Children are keenly aware of spiritual needs. They long for forgiveness in the wake of wrongdoing or failure. They know the pain of breaking promises to themselves and to others. The I'll-never-do-that-again variety of repentance is part of every child's experience. Teens go through turbulent times of sorting out personhood issues and questions surrounding the truth of faith. Young people want to know if God is real, if prayer really works, if the stories of Scripture are fact. Children want to know for themselves whether "Jesus loves me" is more than just a song.

When children are trained to worship, when they are helped to develop as spiritually attuned people, they can begin to encounter God in powerful ways. Counting bricks is no match for a God who longs for our attention. Entertainment is no match for worship. Entertainment fills up our time; worship fits us for eternity.

## Be with Your Children
Paying attention in worship is foundational to training children in the pew. And giving attention to our children during this time is essential. It is very important that parents and children sit together during worship.

On the surface this seems obvious, but many parents find it a relief to let their preschool and older children sit with friends. Children often ask whether they can sit with their pals. When Rob and Scott asked, they were consistently told the reason they needed to stay with me: "It is much harder to pay attention to God when you want to pay attention to your friend. You will have time later to be with your friend; right now Jesus wants all of our attention because he has something to say to us."

There is no substitute for being with your children. During the junior-high years, I let my children know that they could always ask to sit elsewhere and then blame me for denying their request. Sometimes as parents we have to look pretty mean just to help our kids save face. As high-schoolers, the boys now save me a seat or come through the sanctuary to join me, depending on who gets to the sanctuary first after Sunday school.

For parents, being with older teens in worship can seem un-important. But at this age training is increasingly transformed into companionship. This can be the time when expressions of worship take on new depth and meaning. It is important for parents to be a part of a teenager's reflections of faith and truth. If the expectation has been communicated in love and in terms of desire rather than denial, teens are cooperative.

Friends are a very important part of teen life. In most churches there are youth-group teens who attend Sunday services without parents. These kids are usually eager to join other teens and their parents in the pew. So Rob and Scott sit with me in worship and their friends join us.

There may be times when schedules or responsibilities may mean that parents and teens do not end up seated together. But it's best if such times are limited and not allowed to evolve into habitual patterns.

It's true that young people find great security in having rules that don't budge. As Rob and Scott grew up, they simply began to turn down offers to sit away from me, and sometimes they would explain why. More than a few parents of teens have commented on how the boys and I sit together in worship. There is a noticeable affection between us that I treasure and that others see as unusual for teens and parents.

This companionship has not been won without some cost to my own preferences. For example, I love to sing, but I have rarely been able to participate in the church choir. Many choirs are located in the front of the sanctuary, either behind or to the side of the pulpit area. Traditionally, the children of the folks who sing in the choir are not included in the seating. Young children do squirm, scratch, stare and point. They can be distracting if seated in a visible area in front of the congregation. When the choir stands to sing, what do the children do then?

The church my husband pastored for ten years, where my boys grew from infancy to fifth and sixth grade, allowed children to sit with parents who sang in the choir. The sanctuary had some physical flexibility; at one point the choir was moved from the pulpit area to one side of the sanctuary. This provided a place with less potential for distraction. Such flexibility would have been harder to achieve if the choir loft had been a permanent fixture, as it is in many sanctuaries.

When the choir sang, usually the children sat quietly. Most held hymnbooks, as they had been taught to follow along while parents sang. Most of the children who sat in the choir came to church with only one parent. If both parents attended and only one sang in the choir, the children sat with the other parent in the pew. And grandparents could fill the role of this other training parent if necessary.

Seating children with the choir can be more difficult as children get older, for unless they are included as singing members of the choir, they may not want to sit in the choir section. If the choir loft is located in the balcony of a church or in the back, however, I think including children in that seating arrangement poses fewer problems.

Much hinges on the choir director's attitude. If parents in the choir are able to work at training children to worship God, directors should be willing to consider this unorthodox arrangement. Children belong with parents in the pew, and sometimes the pew happens to be in a choir loft.

As children become older and more reticent to sit with the choir, their parents should be free to sit in the congregation and then join the choir for special music. They can sit in an area near the entrance to the loft, and another adult can help children worship during the choir's musical offering to the Lord. In the church where we served during my sons' grade-school years, this arrangement worked because the church was committed to parents' teaching their children to worship. I believe the Lord was glorified by this, and we all agreed to be "humiliated in our own eyes" together.

In another church, I simply decided to sit with my children in the pew and forgo participation in the choir. The logistics of the loft, the preferences of the director and the ages of the boys all contributed to this decision. I've had regrets at times about not being part of the choir, but I have no doubts that I made the right choice. Especially when one of my six-foot sons puts his arm around me in worship and helps me pay attention.

## Being in the Sanctuary

For several years I have had the opportunity to share ideas on parenting in the pew at seminars. Parents are often concerned about the appropriate ages to include children in all or part of the worship service. I usually offer the following age-related guidelines for when children should be included in the worship service, though I recognize that children are different and developmental patterns need to be taken into account.

Older infants and toddlers up to two and a half or three years old do well in the nursery. Nursing infants and older toddlers do well in the service about half of the time. Three-year-olds, and some younger children, can be trained to participate in worship that includes the creed, Scripture readings, music and offering. In most Protestant, evangelical or charismatic congregations, this is a little more than half of a service. By about the fourth year of age, children can be in a service of worship for the entire time.

In our church a sermon just for younger children is included after hymns, readings, choral anthem and creed. Children are asked to come forward and are taught the main point of the upcoming adult sermon in a shorter, more anecdotal way.

Younger children are then given time to leave the sanctuary for supervised toddler activities.

Some churches conduct "children's church" for children well past toddler age. This may or may not include a time of worship. I feel sad when I see children older than four leave for "children's church." Both these children and their parents can miss a lot. I've been eager to guide my sons in worship and have not wanted to give that privilege away to anyone.

But children's church can be very helpful *if it is designed to train children in worship*. Too many children's churches are cut-and-paste times to keep children occupied until the adult service is over. If children are encouraged to leave the service before the "long parts," and this continues into grade school, it's no wonder that older kids balk or succumb to boredom when they are "too old" and have to stay in the sanctuary for the entire "adult service."

Parents must put a positive twist on this incredible privilege. In our home, the fourth birthday was an exceptional celebration. This birthday meant being "old enough" to stay in for the whole service. It was a milestone. Worship is a privilege, and a four-year-old was ready for more. I remember that Scott made the typical second-born request to start early. But he had to wait, and this added to the anticipation and sense of specialness. For a few months after he turned five, Robert felt more elite than ever. After Scott's fourth birthday, it was fun to see his excitement as he remained in the pew after the younger kids went off to children's church. He was finally a "big boy"!

**Being Attentive**

Once you have your children with you in the service, how do

you keep them there? How do you keep them there in mind and spirit as well as in body?

Many kids are allowed to leave at all sorts of times during a service of worship. It is amazing how many young people have to go to the bathroom during church. These are often the same youngsters who can play nine innings of baseball without a pit stop.

Bathroom "emergencies" usually occur during the "long parts" of a service. To keep my children out of the potty parade I did a few simple things. We avoided water-fountain visits between Sunday school and worship. (The attraction of a church water fountain for children is one of life's great mysteries. Water is usually the last thing a kid will drink at home!)

We made a bathroom stop between Sunday school and church. (The aversion kids have for going to the bathroom at logical times is another one of life's mysteries.) The boys knew that going to the bathroom during the worship service was not allowed. Knowing this from the very beginning helped them cooperate about the bathroom visit.

Of course there were exceptions when leaving the sanctuary was allowed. At the sudden onset of a bloody nose or flu symptoms, a parent should accompany the child out to help remedy the situation. Such symptoms are obvious, and every parent knows the difference between the fake and the real thing. It has to do with paleness, clammy hands and what mood the child is in. (It is amazing that these real emergencies occur during the quietest parts of the service, a phenomenon also noticeable with infants who have gas.)

Including children in the worship of God means that some other things need to be excluded. If we want our children to learn to pay attention to the Lord, we will eliminate as many distractions as possible.

This means that toys, loose change, books, Sunday-school papers, pads, pencils, coloring books, dolls and trucks should stay at home. It helps children to be empty-handed except when holding the hymnbook to sing, the bulletin when in use or the Bible during the reading of Scripture. Even tracing the travels of Paul on the maps in the back of the Bible is off-limits except during a sermon detailing Paul's missionary journeys. Kids are quick to think of all sorts of diversions, even religious ones, to pass time in the pew.

Candy, gum or the like to "keep them quiet" is not helpful either. Training children to worship means that they are asked to pay attention and helped to do so. Being quiet comes as they learn to listen and worship, not as they are entertained by games and kept quiet by gum.

Naturally, a child who is being trained to worship can be distracted by other children who are allowed to play in the pew. When Rob and Scott asked why some other children got to color or play with toys in the service, I answered in positive terms about why we were at worship, not in negative terms of why play was not allowed. This helped the boys feel special and not deprived. In general, I always tried to sit away from children who were allowed to have toys and books. As other parents joined me in "parenting in the pew," we sat near each other and helped each other out.

**Being Quiet**
An expectation of paying attention is foundational for learning to worship. Parents sit with their children to help them do this,

but there is more to paying attention than mere proximity will provide.

Simply telling children to "be quiet" is not the way to draw their attention to the worship that is taking place. The purpose of parenting in the pew is to train a child to *worship,* not to be quiet. Quietness at certain times may enhance their ability to worship, but quietness is a means to this effort, not an end.

This distinction is of tremendous importance to a child. It is also a great help to your nerves. It makes sense that when our attention is focused on what is happening in worship with us and with our children, that our own sense of being in God's presence is enriched. If our children's lack of quietness preoccupies us rather than their worship experience, we are simply in the pew in the presence of our kids and are probably feeling far from the presence of God.

But training children to worship does not always enhance our own experience of being before the Lord, especially at first. On a feeling level, the experience of worship may seem impoverished by the demands of parenting in the pew. The number of times children must be helped to concentrate, pay attention and enter into the worship service is almost beyond counting. The effort can be exhausting. And it can be pleasing to God.

It can seem paradoxical that to help a child to develop concentration and a sense of quietness for worship, parents have to talk more. If you sit close to your children, however, you can give whispered instructions and reminders rather easily and with little or no distraction to others.

*Where* parents sit with children can be important. I always tried to avoid sitting too close to "best friends" when the kids were very young. The temptation of distractions was too great

But it can be very helpful to sit near other parents who are training their children to worship. Such parents can understand whispers, share agendas and help each other out. Worship-training parents and friends can encourage each other and pinch-hit for each other as needed. And on a day that goes badly, parents in the pew can remind each other that it's really worth it in the long run.

Helping children pay attention is essential no matter how structured or unstructured a church service may be. All churches have a liturgy. Some are centuries old, some are only as old as a congregation, some are new every Sunday. A liturgy reflects the historical roots of faith as well as a congregation's personal history and preference. The point is to encourage our children's participation in worship, using the liturgy in a way that is appropriate for their ages.

## Being Helpful

Younger worshipers especially need help in learning how to pay attention in worship. Following are some ideas about listening to Scripture and participating in responsive readings and the shorter parts of some liturgies. Chapters to follow will deal fully with music, sermons, prayer and sacraments.

In the story of Jeremy, the little boy with a dog named Precious, I have illustrated how exciting paying attention can be when a four-year-old participates in the responsive reading. I helped Jeremy, as I had helped my own boys, by allowing him to stand on the pew as I stood. This brought him up high enough that I could easily put my arm around him and hold the hymnbook that contained the reading in front of him. For toddlers, this stance also adds a measure of what I call "affectionate control." You are holding your child very close, but in a way that is more of a hug than a tug.

Then, as most toddlers know their colors, I was able to point to the words as we went along. In our responsive reading tradition, the pastor reads the black print and the congregation the red print. I told Jeremy to watch my finger as it pointed to "the black words that 'Uncle' Breck would read" and to listen carefully. I told him to watch my finger point to the red words and listen again. This method helps children to pay attention through sight as well as through hearing.

A similar method can be used when responsive readings aren't marked off by color differences. Some responsive readings are differentiated by type style or by headings. The point is to draw children to pay attention by helping them focus on what is happening and listen carefully to what is being said.

As soon as children are able to read even a few words, ask them to read the words they recognize and to listen to the meaning. As soon as children can read well, they can hold their own books and probably stand on the floor rather than on the pew. Older children should be able to identify the Scripture source for the responsive reading or the history of some alternative reading for a particular Sunday.

If children are trained to participate at a young age, their sense of belonging and paying attention is more natural. I am very saddened by the number of older children and teens I see just standing up looking bored through parts of the service that they could participate in if they were asked.

During the reading of the Scripture, a bit of creativity can help children to listen well. If the reading is a narrative or story, young children can be asked to pretend that they were really

there when the action took place. Parents can draw attention
to the content of Scripture as it is read by questions: "How do
you think Jesus looked or sounded when he said this?" "How
would you feel if you had been there?" "What does this Scripture say about how you felt yesterday?"

These questions are asked to get the child thinking. The child
may respond with a whispered word or phrase, or you may want
to wait until you have left the sanctuary before picking up the
question again. As children are trained, they get the idea of how
and when to respond. Worship situations and sanctuaries vary,
but children who are responding to the service are far less distracting to others than children who are allowed to play in the pew.

With teens, questions about tone—"if this Scripture were a
movie scene"—or something pertinent to their lives can be helpful. Let teens make comments to you as they make connections
between Scripture readings and their lives.

Children will often get more out of Scripture readings than
you had expected. Sometimes they will hear a passage of Scripture for the first time in a worship service, and they will respond
honestly. This can lead to some fascinating discussions about
plagues, fire, how the Holy Spirit really operates and many
other topics. Kids have been known to want revenge big-time
when they hear about Herod, Judas Iscariot or other biblical
"bad guys."

Questions are good for children, and they are briefer than
explanations in a worship service that keeps moving along as
you parent in the pew. You usually will have time to ask only
one question or make one comment to draw attention to each
part of worship as it happens.

When we ask our children to pay attention, we often end up

doing a better job of it ourselves. It is not unusual for parents to express delight as their own sense of worship is enhanced through practicing parenting in the pew. The liturgy becomes less routine and more relevant. Not because the words have changed, but because we listen again to the familiar and find that God is still speaking.

## Being Firm

Parenting in the pew goes better some weeks than others, for as many reasons as there are parents and kids. Being consistent is never easy. We all get tired. But I have been more consistent in worship training than in other parenting tasks. I think that has been so because it means more to me than other things, even food.

Being determined, however, does not preclude turmoil. As I began to share with parents what I had learned about parenting in the pew, I asked the boys what had helped them the most: "What is the one thing I did that helped you more than anything to appreciate the importance of learning to worship?" They were about ten and eleven at the time. I asked each boy privately, out of the other's hearing. Much to my surprise, they gave an identical answer. I wasn't thrilled with their response, but I was the one who had asked. "Oh, Mama," each of them said, "it was the morning you marched me out and spanked my behind!"

My only consolation was that each testified that this was a singular happening, but they knew I was serious from that time on. They went on to say that what followed the spanking—my earnest lecture on God's desire for their love and attentiveness—helped too.

I want to emphasize that there are big differences between

kids, and differences in the way parents train their kids. Many parents refrain from corporal punishment and find other effective means to influence the behavior of their children. Sadly, some parents find it hard to control the extent of corporal punishment, and abuse results. Spanking can be counterproductive for some children. A privilege denied or another consequence may be just as motivating to some children. But empty threats and parental frustration are never much help at all.

Whatever communicates to your child that you are serious about behavior in certain situations, whether it is the supermarket or the sanctuary, should be applied in private and with consistency. Being clear about expectations and consequence is very important, no matter how children are disciplined.

Robert and Scott received the discipline of spanking and were responsive to its intent. I am glad those days are over. Mom was right; it does hurt the parent more. I don't know why exactly Rob and Scott spoke of this as the most helpful part of their training. But I would be less than honest if I left this story out.

Proverbs 22 includes admonitions to parents to "train a child in the way he should go" (v. 6) and to use corporal discipline wisely (v. 15), and follows this advice with

Pay attention and listen to the sayings of the wise;
    apply your heart to what I teach,
for it is pleasing when you keep them in your heart
    and have all of them ready on your lips.
*So that your trust may be in the LORD,*
    I teach you today, even you. (vv. 17-19)

Parenting in the pew is not easy, but I am grateful to have children that know they can count on the God they have encountered. It beats counting bricks.

# Make
# a Joyful
# Noise

# 6

T he Atomic Praise Choir at our church was in full
swing! Junior-high and high-school kids were enthusiastic about wearing tie-dyed T-shirts, tucked in,
with blue jeans (no holes). They liked singing new hymns of the
church, praise choruses and songs by artists heard on Christian
radio.

"Atomic Praise" was a name cooked up in a brainstorming
session. The idea was that this choir wanted to praise God with
"every molecule" of their lives. Enthusiasm was high. As the
choir director I could carry a tune, but barely read music. I just

wanted the church youth, Rob and Scott included, to discover what it might mean to worship the Lord with music. It was parenting in the pew on a massive scale.

The kids welcomed the challenge from the beginning. I let them know the rules up front. The girls couldn't believe I was serious about "no writing or passing notes." They all blinked when I told them they had to pay attention to the service. They sat up straight when I told them that we would have a test on the sermon every week at practice! (I'll tell you more about this in chapter eight.)

The thing that made it all worthwhile to them was the idea that we were not going to perform for a congregational audience, but praise God directly with our hearts and voices. Teenage molecules matter to the Lord. And music matters to teens. Putting the two together was a way to worship God with new insight and enthusiasm.

### Music and Teenagers

Doctrine, theology and the definitions to unfamiliar words are pretty far down on the list of teen interests. Good Christian music, new and old, gives an opportunity to teach the truth of our faith in a way that is more interesting to teenagers. The secular world certainly advertises its message through countless earphones plugged into adolescent audiophiles.

The Atomic Praise Choir discussed the message in the music. One Christmas we talked about what it meant for God to become "a man lost in time and space without rank or place." We talked about *atonement, redemption, hosanna* and *alleluia.* What do these words mean—not just in the dictionary, but in our hearts?

The most difficult thing for many teens is allowing the truths they learn in their heads to influence their real lives and behaviors. So many live compartmentalized lives. There is "church behavior" and then there is the-rest-of-the-world behavior. Within a downbeat after the last note of "Brother, Let Me Be Your Servant," the choir members' verbal putdown games would begin.

Sometimes with calm and patience and sometimes with an explosion of emotion, I would draw attention to this hypocrisy. Sometimes they listened. Sometimes they tuned me out. My efforts in practice to prepare them for worship were not in vain, but it was the experience of worship itself that meant the most.

Teenagers need to worship the Lord. When they are confronted by a reality beyond themselves, a reality that stands against the relativism of their culture, teens are comforted. The absolutes of the gospel revealed to us in Jesus Christ offer security and true freedom to teens living in a seductive world that tells them anything and everything just to make a sale. God's Word is not a sales pitch. It is the Truth. Worship gives teens a chance to meet the Truth-Teller "up-close and personal." Music is a good way to make the introduction.

However, introductions are best made one by one rather than on the mass scale I attempted with Atomic Praise. Through advocacy and interest, parents of teens can help their increasingly independent children worship through music. Listen to contemporary Christian music with your teens. Talk about words and meanings. Some of this music is fluff and meaningless repetition. But much of it contains new-wineskin insights of how the gospel relates to the world today.

Talk about the older hymns of the church. Define words and

discuss meanings. Again, some of this music is fluff and meaningless repetition. But many hymns, the "oldies but goodies"
that have lasted for centuries, distill the gospel into rhymes of
truth. All hymns, whether written two years or two centuries
ago, were new once.

J. S. Bach and Michael W. Smith have both expressed in
music what the Holy Spirit has set in their hearts. Both can lead
us to the throne of grace in worship. Talk to your pastor, worship leader, music director or worship committee about including a variety of sounds in sacred music.

Ethnic variety as well as style and generational variety helps
us express before the Lord what the kingdom of God is all
about. The kingdom is young and old, from every tribe and
nation. Teenagers, with their appetite for change and newness,
can help an entire congregation better reflect the biblical kingdom that transcends cultures, generations and personal preferences.

### Starting Young Helps
Teenagers were all toddlers once upon a time. Parents of
toddlers think the high-school years will never come, while parents of teens think toddlerdom was just the day before yesterday. In all the seasons of childhood, there is music.

Jesus loves me, this I know;
For the Bible tells me so.

This is a toddler standard. It was also the reply of twentieth-
century theologian Karl Barth when asked to summarize the
essence of his faith. Truth can be learned to a tune played with
two fingers. Barth argued for the revelatory nature of biblical
authority in an extremely sophisticated and learned manner.

Toddlers boom it out in church basements every Sunday.

Music is one of the easier tools for parents to use in teaching their children to worship. Music is prescribed in Scripture as a means to worship (Psalm 33:3, Psalm 100:2 and Colossians 3:16 are just a few examples). In the next chapter I will discuss how praise and prayer are often expressed through music. Scripture memorizing, too, is made easier if done through songs.

Sunday-school music, however, is seldom the music of the sanctuary. Parents need help in getting the youngest of worshipers to sing praise to God through music written for adults. This can be a significant way that young children are connected to the heritage and history of the church. Worship music can also lay a foundation for understanding the truth of God that produces the theologians of the next century.

Training children to sing hymns and songs in the sanctuary is one of the easiest aspects of parenting in the pew. Children love being set free to "make a joyful noise." This opportunity is not to be missed!

During songs or hymns, encourage very young children to sing "la, la, la" with the tune if the words are totally unknown or unpronounceable to them. Children don't mind doing this and will quickly begin to pick up the refrain or a repeated phrase.

Children can learn hymns more easily if a certain one is sung several weeks in a row. A "hymn of the month" can be a great help to parents in the pew, especially those with preschoolers who as yet lack reading skills. If you think this would be helpful, ask your pastor, music director or worship committee to consider this as a ministry for the training of children. Even adults without children in the pew may not mind the repetition if it is seen as purposeful.

It is especially helpful for teens to know the history behind
the writing of a hymn. Many classical as well as contemporary
hymns have a story behind them that can enhance any worship-
er's sense of reverence and joy, but especially teenagers who
often question the relevance of traditions. The pastor or worship leader can tell these stories to the congregation. Also, many
church libraries have books that give the stories behind the
hymns and their authors.

It is important to help children feel physically involved in
worship. Even before they can read, they need to be able to hold
a hymnbook or see the overhead screen. This usually means that
toddlers and early-grade-schoolers stand on the pew or chair
next to their parent. The parent stands with one arm around the
child, either holding the hymnbook or helping draw attention
to the screen.

The parent should try to sing in such a way that the child can
hear the song clearly, and when necessary the parent can give
instructions. As a "single" parent between two children, I used
one hymnbook for the three of us. One of the boys held the
book while I pointed out the words with one finger, stanza by
stanza. My other arm usually found itself around the child who
wiggled the most that Sunday.

After they could read fairly well, each of the boys held a
hymnbook and I would sing out of one or the other. If your
church uses an overhead screen, the same close-standing and
directive methods can be used, but remember that it is harder
for children to concentrate visually. They can be instructed and
encouraged to listen even more attentively to the words.

Very young children can be asked to listen for a particular
word or phrase in a song. They will join in with gusto as they

catch on. One of my fondest memories of worship with my toddlers came during the singing of "Ask Ye What Great Thing I Know." After three or four lines the declarative refrain is "Jesus Christ, the Crucified!" What a time my boys had waiting and listening for this line. At first I had to give them a cue— a nod of my head or a loudly whispered "Now!"—and they would sing out with toddler enthusiasm the joyous refrain.

As children get older, it's good to explain and discuss the content of hymns. This can be done prior to worship as you are settled in the pew. It can also be done at home with familiar hymns and in more informal times. Brief insights or meaning can be highlighted during the instrumental introduction to the song or hymn. Good worship leaders will often help the congregation focus on the content or worship intention of church music, and parents can direct children to listen to and understand these explanations.

Always the integrity of heart and voice, of believing what is being sung, is important in worship. Some songs contain declarations that we would like to be true of us, but may highlight hypocrisy or shortcomings in our lives instead. We need to be able to talk about our struggle to "surrender all" to Jesus. We need to help our children understand that grace really *is* amazing—that once being lost and now being found, being blind and now seeing, are not just words to a song, but the testimony of what it means to be known by Jesus.

This can often be accomplished through simple, whispered expressions that help a child or teen know what you are thinking after a hymn is sung. I've often done this as we sat back in the pew after singing. "Jesus was sure my friend this week when I was worried about Grandpa" can enhance the meaningfulness

of "What a Friend We Have in Jesus." Such remarks help
children get the idea that what is sung really matters; it really
counts in everyday life as well as Sunday worship. They learn
to listen to the words they sing. They learn to live the words
too.

## Listening to Others' Music

Worship services often contain offerings of music that are not
intended for the congregation's direct participation. Choral offertories and anthems are sung to God, while the congregation
is invited to worship in a meditative way as the music leads.
Young children can be taught to listen for a special word within
a choral selection. They can squeeze your hand every time they
hear the word *Jesus* or *glory,* for instance. In this way they learn
to listen, pay attention and appreciate the words as well as the
music. This is a helpful skill for older children who may not
prefer the style of music but can listen for truth in the lyrics.

Some music—instrumental preludes, offertories and post-
ludes—is offered to the Lord without words. Children can be
asked to listen closely and picture what is going on in the music.
Parents can ask the child to think of a Bible story that seems
to go along with the music. Not surprisingly, children find this
quite easy to do. It may not be what the composer had in mind
or match the piece's title in any way, but children "see" action
in their imaginations suggested by the music. In worship, children can be reminded to think about God, creation, a Bible story
or other sacred things as they listen. Is the music happy? sad?
peaceful? turbulent? Children reared in the age of video have no
problems thinking in pictures to music. Classical music is the
background of choice for many cartoons.

To help children concentrate on sacred music, especially older music, in worship, it is wise to practice with wordless classical music. A great place to do this with less boredom and distraction is in the car. I began to train Rob and Scott in listening to all sorts of instrumental music when driving. I'd tune in a classical station or put in an instrumental cassette. Then I'd ask them to listen and think what kind of story or movie scene could happen to this music. In the sanctuary, where worship is the point, I usually suggested a general idea or theme, but in the car I did not. They could come up with anything—and they did! Great fugues were the backgrounds for shark attacks and car races. Quieter pieces were ladybugs in the grass or sneaky spies creeping up on someone. It was fun. And it helped.

In church the prelude might begin to remind them of Jesus when he fed the multitude. A lively offertory might be God creating the dinosaurs. It may not be what Handel (or whoever) had in mind, but the boys were learning to listen. It was a start.

This last Easter season, our church choir led the congregation in a special Holy Thursday service. Most of the music was offered to the Lord by the choir alone. At the close of worship, we were to file out in silence as the sanctuary was darkened. Scott just sat back in the pew and whispered for me to go ahead. "I just want to sit here for a few minutes and think about stuff," he said. I was so grateful that he had learned to listen to music in worship.

## Children's Choir

Children's choirs can be of great help in including young people's gifts in worship. Encourage your children to participate as an offering to God, not to perform for the congregation. Verbally reinforce this both before and after the service. Compliments can focus less on how the child did than on how worship was enhanced or how God was blessed.

"I really thought a lot about how God loves me while you sang your song to the Lord this morning. Thank you for helping me worship." This comment is very different from "Oh, I was so proud of you this morning. You sang so well." Children will hear the difference, and they will be reminded of what is important in worship. They will learn the vast difference between school programs and leading others into the presence of the living God.

The temptation to take pictures or video-record children's choirs in worship should be resisted. And congregations that use clapping as an expression of gratitude to God should be careful to teach children the difference between applause focused on a performance and the clapping of hands offered as praise to God.

### Ain't No Rock!

There is a song I like to sing to the Lord that comes from Jesus' warning that if people do not praise him, the rocks will. This song also reflects on the psalms that declare that all creation gives praise to the Lord. Birds sing, trees wave their branches.

This song, with its very old sentiment, is put to a contemporary beat, sort of an old gospel spiritual sound. It is a joy to sing. My family has heard me sing at the top of my lungs:

Ain't no rock gonna cry in my place,
As long as I'm alive
To glorify his holy name!

Ain't no tree gonna wave its branches,
I'll lift my hands
To glorify his holy name!
Ain't no bird gonna sing in my place,
I'll lift my voice
To glorify his holy name!
Oh, I'm gonna praise his holy name!
As long as I'm alive
To glorify his holy name!

(LaMarquis Jefferson, © 1987 Integrity's Praise Music)
Beyond its Scripture-based message, there is probably plenty to
criticize about this song. The double negatives alone would
make most English teachers scowl. But this song draws me to
"glorify God and enjoy him forever," which the Shorter Cate-
chism tells me is my "chief end."

In teaching children how to worship we must remind them
that their "chief end" is the glory of God. We need to make a
joyful noise before the Lord in worship. We need to "sing to the
Lord a new song." We need to show our children what it means
to begin to enjoy the Lord forever.

And our children need to enter into the heritage of faith left
to us by songwriters in ages past.

What language shall I borrow
To thank Thee, dearest friend,
For this Thy dying sorrow,
Thy pity without end?
O make me Thine forever;
And should I fainting be,
Lord, let me never, never
Outlive my love to Thee. (Bernard of Clairvaux, 1091-1153)

# Prayer,
# Confession and
# Canned Goods

# 7

My mother tells me that when I was very young, I had an invisible friend named Werff. She remembers that this creature was very small, very near, and that I was adamant about where Werff was, what he liked to eat and things I heard him say. Werff was occasionally stepped on, sat on or inadvertently interrupted, but my friend always recovered. Werff seems to have disappeared somewhere, though, when my sister Kellie was born.

Children have the capacity to speak to and listen to what is unseen. The faith they possess to do so is part of what Jesus commended as the very faith that gives evidence of the kingdom of God. Children can know what it is to pray in faith to an unseen God who is a real friend.

If our children learn to pray, to speak to God and to hear him speak to them, a solid foundation of faith can be set in their lives. And because God is real and well able to establish communication with our children, he will not fade away like imaginary childhood friends.

### Praying, Not Parroting

Parents, pastors and Christian educators often do not give children enough opportunities to enter into the prayer life of church or home. Children may be taught to "say grace" and "God-bless-so-and-so," but little else. Children need to be trained to pray and not parrot Christian phrases. Saying grace and praying "God bless" are not necessarily parroting, but they can be if these prayers are taught the same way as lines to a kindergarten play or how to say "please" and "thank you."

Children can be taught to pray by entering at an early age into the uncertainties as well as the joys of prayer. I remember one night Robert was wheezing with asthma. As a seven-year-old, he struggled with the idea that Jesus *could* heal, but had not healed him. After many prayers of his own, along with ours and those of the elders of the church, Robert surprised me with a faith that I sometimes struggled to reach myself. Between heavy breaths, he prayed: "Jesus, I know that you know best. I sure would like to be better, but whatever you do is okay with me."

About a year later, Robert prayed the night before my husband had to have knee surgery, "Dear Jesus, please make Daddy's knee all better so when the doctors see it tomorrow they will be surprised that they don't have to fix it. Well, I know you always do what's best, so if you decide not to do what I really want, well, that's . . ." He paused and then haltingly and deliberately continued, "okay . . . because . . . you . . . are still . . . well . . . Jesus."

Scripture is full of wonderful stories of heart's-desire prayers answered. It is also full of honest disappointment in prayer. Children can handle both. If prayer is to become real to children, if God is to become real to them, faith must find its foundation in real-life experiences with God in prayer. God must be trusted to say yes or no as he determines how best to love us.

## Home Training for Corporate Prayer
Structures for different types of prayer can be found in the corporate worship of the church. Most liturgies contain times for confession, intercession and praise. These times of congregational prayer are an important part of training children to trust God with their lives and to know the needs and support of God's greater family.

A crucial element of preparing children for congregational prayer is prayer in the home. From the earliest age children should be encouraged to speak to God in their own words. You can probably teach them best by sharing prayers in your own words with them. Children need to hear their parents "just talk" to God. They need to see us, and sit with us eventually, as we listen to God in silence.

Prayer needs to be woven into the fabric of our lives. Children need to see that prayer is central to our faith-filled dependence upon God. They need to see that prayer is not frivolous wishing-with-amen-at-the-end. I don't pray for parking spots just because I'm running late. But my children have heard me pray for a parking spot on a busy street in front of the doctor's office when Scott had a 105-degree temperature and it was pouring rain. And they've been able to *marvel* in the New Testament sense when we parked in that spot!

## Honesty in Prayer

Scott prayed one night when he was four, "Jesus, thank you for all the beautiful things in the world, and all the canned goods." This is how I found out about the collection for canned goods in the Sunday school! Scott was also famous for being grateful for chicken as a toddler. It was his favorite food. Still is.

Children need to talk to God about the things that concern their lives. As parents, we need to be honest about situations in our world and our lives that we do not understand. Children have a sense about what is real or not real to us.

Most children get suspicious at an early age about the actual existence of Santa Claus and the tooth fairy. God needs to be in a different category! In fact, though a full discussion of this topic goes beyond the scope of this book, I will admit that we never did practice traditions of fantasy-as-fact in our home. Santa Claus was treated like Donald Duck, a person in costume with a made-up story. We did not keep most of the traditions of our culture that have come to be associated with the holidays of the church. Whether or not other parents do as we did, it is important for our kids to sense a clear difference between Jesus and the Easter Bunny.

God is believable because he is real. His reality rings true with children because of his sovereignty. God's purposes and will do not always match our expectations. It is very often in disappointment or difficulty in the lives of our children that God's existence becomes objective and real, distinctive and powerful for them. We shouldn't be afraid that prayer that is not answered according to our hopes will weaken or destroy our children's faith. Children need to see that God can be trusted no matter what. This is the foundation for maturing faith.

Recently, a college student lived a short while with a family in our church. She needed some shelter and encouragement after a particularly difficult emotional crisis. The family she stayed with does a very good job of prayer and Scripture training in their home (and worship training in the pew!). While staying with this family, the student lost her job. After family prayers for her predicament, the six-year-old sought out the weeping, fearful student. This little child of faith put her arm around her sad "big sister" and told her matter-of-factly, "You know God knew about this day even before you were born. So if he knows all about it and it's okay with him, well, it will be okay."

The student was able to share with me and with the couple she was staying with that Psalm 139 was never more real to her than in the confident understanding of this very young child. Such is the kingdom. Learning to pray about real things, simple or profound, prepares children to participate in the church family.

The church needs to hear the prayers of children, because they often reflect the best definition of faith given in the Scripture: "Faith is being sure of what we hope for and certain of what we do not see" (Hebrews 11:1).

## Prayer for Grubby Hearts

Forgiveness is one of our most hoped-for yet unseen needs in life. It is realized through faith that finds expression in prayers of confession. In worship services, prayers of confession are usually followed by the pastor or worship leader's declaration of forgiveness, using a promise of Scripture. This can be an important experience for a child.

During prayers that include a time for personal silent confession, very young children should probably be guided by quiet whispers. It goes something like this, "Now is the time we bow our heads and talk to Jesus about stuff we are sorry about. Remember our talk this morning about being selfish? Tell Jesus about this now, and ask him to help you share the last doughnut next time."

One confession dear to my heart (and I'm sure to God's) went something like this, "Dear Jesus, you cleaned up my heart last week and now it is all grubby again. I need some help!" I bet the sermon that week was from Romans 7. I do know that this young grade-schooler was learning to talk honestly with the Lord.

A toddler can be encouraged to confess any recent "no-no," but it should be something that he or she actually remembers, something that is not more than a day old. Fortunately for purposes of training in confession, this is not a problem for the normal toddler! But should children come to worship with a "clean slate," confession time can be used as a time to "thank Jesus for loving us no matter what."

## Prayer for Patience

As we parent our children to love God, we need to guard against charging every situation with a deeply spiritual lesson. "Don't judge October apples in June" was probably the best advice I ever received as a young mother concerned with the willfulness of one of my toddlers. It is a mark of our own maturing faith in God *not* to try to play Holy Spirit in the lives of our children.

True repentance, genuine spiritual insight and real faith are the fruits of the Holy Spirit's work in our lives and the lives of our children. The apostle Paul reminds us, "For we are God's workmanship, created in Christ Jesus to do good works, which God prepared in advance for us to do" (Ephesians 2:10).

The longing in our hearts for our kids to "turn out right" can cause us to make a mountain out of every molehill in our child's life. Every scratch, sneeze, milk spill or childish sin is not an occasion for a sermon or spiritual lesson. Sometimes it's hard to relax with our own kids. It can be difficult to see the humor in their antics, even though we laugh about the same things done by other people's kids.

Parenting can be stressful. Especially if we try to take on God's job as well as our own. And it is God's job to be working in the lives of our children.

God's work is lasting, wise, patient and all-knowing. We parents, no matter how well we succeed at times, fall short in all four categories. He alone is the perfect Parent who loves our children perfectly. We must trust him to be at work in the lives of our children, even when this is hard to do.

As our children grow, they need to confess sin as they see it. Prayers need to become increasingly filled with the concerns they bring up. We need to trust the Lord with the spiritual growth of our children. I believe that God is writing a testimony in the lives of our children. It is his story. He alone sees the end from the beginning. He alone sees the "October apples" when it is only June.

## Prayer in the Church

Prayer that is specific, concrete and arising from real-life situations fosters an honesty with God that can lead to a lifetime of experiencing redemption and grace. This kind of praying by children can encourage the same kind of realness and honesty in the prayer life of our churches. Corporate prayer in the church is all too often superficial and filled with parrotlike religious phrases.

"Dear God, don't let Tommy get killed in the war" was the prayer on all of our hearts but on none of our adult lips one Sunday—until a child said it for us. Sunday-school teachers and trusted friends need to pray with the child who blurts out one morning, "My daddy has a girlfriend and doesn't love us anymore." The honest prayers of children remind us that our Father knows all the details, all the struggle, all the answers.

Many children are the masters of details that we soon forget—or wish we could! Training children in prayers of intercession can be an adventure in remembering. Young children who hear about someone in the church who is very ill will remember to pray for that person even when we don't. This is especially true if they are allowed to visit the sick person.

When visiting does not hinder the well-being of the ill person, children can often be the very best of visitors. Such visits are usually brief and followed by a million questions, especially if they take place in the hospital. Much information about expectations should be given before the visit, and patient explanations are needed afterward. Seeing the sick person, feeling a part of his or her experience, helps children from toddlers to teens to pray with more care, insight and genuine faith. And the sick person is usually glad for an honest visitor who wants to know "what that is" and doesn't just make small talk.

Prayer is a major part of being a church family. Our children need to be a part of our relationships within that family. The answers God gives us as a family of faith are his way of loving us and encouraging our trust.

It all starts with little things. Teaching very young children to fold their hands and close their eyes is a way to enhance their ability to concentrate on what they are doing. These gestures are not prayer in and of themselves, but a means to that end. They need to be taught, shown, retaught and explained in that context.

## Prayer for the World

Prayer must be more than ritual and gesture for our children and young people. Teaching children to pray for the mission concerns of the church can be enhanced by real-life visits from people from the country in which a church has a missionary or a mission concern. Very often an inquiry with the international student office at a local university can put the church in contact with students from all over the world. Lonely international students are more than eager to be invited to meet others and tell about their home and culture. Sometimes these students are not Christian, and your initiative in reaching out can spark friendships and opportunities to share the gospel.

International Christians should be given opportunities to pray with congregations in their native language. What a vivid reminder that God loves the whole world and listens to prayer in any language.

Our children have been influenced greatly by the international students who have been invited into our home and churches.
They know the world is broader than their own hometown,
their geography skills are excellent, and they will eat just about
anything. And they pray for others around the world with a
fondness and warmth that is radically different from the prej-
udice and isolationism found in many teens outside the church.

## Prayers of Praise

Praise is one of the easier aspects of prayer for children to learn.
Expressions of thanks come fairly easily for young people. If
traditional hymns are used in liturgy, very often one will be a
hymn of praise. Point this out to your children. Seeing prayer
in the lyrics can be an important help as you teach your children
to praise God.

Helping children identify a truth about God's character can
help children learn to praise God for who he is. A hymn, a
sermon illustration or a phrase in a creed can highlight a characteristic of God. This can be used to help children focus on a
single aspect of God and to give thanks.

Current events in congregational life can also bring into focus
how God's character affects our daily life. Recently a family in
our church lost their home in a fire. In the worship service,
thanksgiving was given for God's safekeeping. Mention was
made of God's presence and power at work in waking a family
member before any smoke entered the bedroom areas of the
home. That morning we sang hymns that confessed God as
sovereign, God as a hiding place and God as the giver of peace.
This was a good opportunity for parents in the congregation to
help their children focus on the character of God and to give

the Lord praise for making himself so evident in the lives of people they knew.

Drawing children to a life of praise and gratitude is vital in a world so full of discontent and restlessness. One four-year-old in our church dissolved in quiet tears during a praise song one Sunday. The Scriptures tell us that the Holy Spirit helps us pray with "groans that words cannot express." Little Sarah was moved by the music and words of a sung prayer of praise. Her tears were the purest expression of prayer. Her mom held her quietly and shared that moment with her, reassuring her that it was a good way to feel toward God. Once this same little one had misbehaved and I had heard her whisper, "Oh Mommy, don't take me out." To stay, to be a part, to be involved in the worship of God is important to Sarah. She is learning that her presence and her parents are important parts of that experience.

## Teens in Prayer

Until high-school days, we had devotions with prayer and Bible reading as a family each morning before we were off to school and work. We used devotional guides at times. The series from Youth for Christ is especially well written and doesn't talk down to kids. Harold Shaw Publishers has a series of Bible study guides for teens that we used for an evening study.

As high-school days started, the boys began to have a "devo" in the morning on their own, with Bible readings they chose themselves. Some days were better than others. They had to be reminded. The boys began to learn how different a day could be depending on whether or not they had spent time with the Lord. After personal "devo" time, we would have family prayer together. This practice was enhanced by a summer experience in the wilderness with Teen Missions International. The spiritual richness of an extended time each morning in prayer and Scripture was one of the main reasons the boys signed up for a second summer.

Teenagers in a charismatic community can begin to embrace expressions of faith that are evident in their parents and congregations, like speaking in tongues and the laying on of hands. With all types of churches and kids, there are seasons of spirituality that must be encountered and entrusted to God. Raising hands and using "tongues" in praise are important to parents in some charismatic and Pentecostal communities. Parents who worship in this tradition naturally want their children to share in these expressions.

Smaller children will often cheerfully imitate what they see, and parents then simply need to teach them the meaning and practice of these traditions. Many parents become concerned, however, when junior-high and older young people back off and become more guarded in their outward participation.

For kids of all denominational stripes, the teen years are a typical time to step back and evaluate why they are doing what they are doing. This can be a wonderful time for us parents to share our histories and stories of faith. But we also need to share stories of failure. Sometimes the latter will be more encouraging to a young person who is struggling with doubts and questions. This can be the stuff of grown-up prayer. David's psalms of paradoxical doubt and faith can help teens stay close to the Lord in times of struggle. (See Psalms 10, 13, 40 and 142 for examples.)

Teens need to begin to own their own faith. Their expressions of faith need to come increasingly from their hearts and less from helps parents have provided. The gifts of the Spirit are truly *gifts*. This is the time when they need to open up their lives and hearts in the way the Spirit directs. We parents will not always see what we want to see in our children's lives, but then God's ways are not our ways.

Let hands be raised, expressions of gifts come forth and works of service be offered as the Lord directs. Our children need to be with us in the pew. Hearing God's Word can touch their hearts and teach them in ways we cannot see.

We need to pray for our teens. A lot. They need to know about our struggles of faith. This will do more to help them share their struggles with us and with the Lord than almost anything else.

Teens also need to be encouraged to take risks, costly risks, for the Lord. Short-term summer missions to places of challenge and deprivation can be the very best training experiences in prayer. Prayer is what it should be when there are no options. Out of teens' own experience with God in the pew or in Peru, God can fashion young men and women who love him with all their hearts.

### Prayers of Silence

Learning to listen in prayer is hard for all of us in a very noisy society. Our silence, however, gives God a chance to get a word in edgewise. Training in silence can be introduced in the later teen years, but even as they are growing up children need to know that silence is an important part of their parents' prayer life. And if listening in prayer is a "growing edge" for you, maybe you can grow with your teen in this regard.

When Rob and Scott were fifteen and sixteen, I began to

teach them about letting Scripture enhance the practice of silence in prayer. I took advantage of an opportunity when they had seen a group of college students practice this form of prayer, so they were very receptive. (Parents need to expose teens to alternative mentors in the faith. It is good to listen to teens and pick up on who are the people of faith who communicate well with them. College students are big for my kids.)

For our first "retreat of silence," the two boys and I sat in a quiet room together and asked the Lord to bring to each of our minds a story about Jesus from Scripture. It could be any story, I reassured them. When one came to mind, I told them just to sit there and try to visualize the place, sounds, scene, people and Jesus. As they lingered in the scene, I asked each of them to pray silently and invite the Lord to teach them something as they revisited this biblical event.

For our first attempt at silence in prayer, I limited the time to twelve minutes. As they listened for God's voice, I silently asked the Lord to speak a word of grace and truth to my sons.

I was shocked (O ye of little faith!) to find out that God took just those twelve minutes to put his finger on some of the deepest issues of faith and obedience in their lives. I had never heard Rob and Scott reflect more clearly on what God was seeking to do in their lives. That first experience of God's "talking back" in prayer helped them begin to discern his voice as distinct from their own. I have not continued regular sessions of silent prayer with my boys, but sometimes I have chosen and read a particular Scripture and helped them use their five senses to enter imaginatively into the biblical scene.

Many young people ask, "How do you hear God speak to you? How do you tell that it is God?" The answer is necessarily ineffable. It is something you *know* deeply and distinctly. Using Scripture to guide this kind of listening in prayer is helpful. It is especially important for young Christians, and for teens who tend to be emotional in how they perceive God's direction and nearly everything else.

The thing that struck me after that first attempt at silent meditation in prayer was how *easy* it was for Rob and Scott. I realized that the boys were able to concentrate quite easily on the Scripture-scene because they had been trained from their early years to listen intently and vividly to the reading of Scripture and its exposition in sermons.

Parenting in the pew has helped my children in more ways than I ever could imagine. It's almost September, and I am beginning to see my October apples mature.

# Just How Long Was That Sermon?

# 8

Eutychus is definitely the patron saint of everyone who has fallen asleep during a sermon. His story is recorded in the book of Acts:

Seated in a window was a young man named Eutychus, who was sinking into a deep sleep as Paul talked on and on. When he was sound asleep, he fell to the ground from the third story and was picked up dead. Paul went down, threw himself on the young man and put his arms around him. "Don't be alarmed," he said. "He's alive!" . . . The people took the young man home alive and were greatly comforted. (Acts 20:9-10, 12)

There is more than a little instruction for parents in this story. The first is that Eutychus should never have been sitting on the window sill. He should have been with his parents in the pew. He might have still fallen asleep (Paul's sermon started at sundown on Sunday and didn't end until midnight!), but it would have caused less commotion. Actually, probably more than a few people present secretly welcomed the unfortunate distraction. As it was, Paul just put his arms around the boy, pronounced him alive and then picked up his sermon where he left off, preaching on "until daybreak" (v. 11)!

This story is a valuable one to keep in mind the next time your kids complain about sermons being too long. Let them know it could be longer, even lethal. But of greater help to parents is Paul's encouragement, "Don't be alarmed; he's alive!"

The "don't be alarmed" part, of course, comes easily for a single man who has no children. Nevertheless, we parents are to take heart! There is not a saint alive that has managed to stay awake during every sermon she or he ever heard.

The different personalities and attention spans of children make a wide variety of behaviors possible when the "long part" of the worship service begins. Concentrating on the sermon is one of the hardest parts of worship for children of all ages—even when Daddy is the preacher. Helping children listen to and learn from the sermon takes persistence, creativity and time. It also helps to have a pastor who thinks of children as well as adults as the sermon is prepared.

### Tuning In Young Children

Very young children need their attention drawn to the parts of a sermon that are illustrative. "Listen to this story" is a way of directing attention to parts of the sermon that can be most easily understood by youngsters.

Jesus told parables because a picture really is worth a thousand words; for most of us, stories are easier to grasp than abstractions. Pastors often use illustrations to help make a point they want their flock to take home. All people—but especially children—remember stories.

Short sermons just for children are often included as a part of worship. Often grade-school and younger children are asked to come forward to sit near the front for a special message. Pastors may use this time to share the truth of Scripture with the youngest parishioners.

The children's sermon works best if it relates directly to the "adult sermon" that usually comes later in the worship service. This is a good opportunity for the pastor to tell a story or give an illustration that relates to children's lives and also to a major point of the day's sermon. Children's sermons need to deal with real issues and questions of faith in the lives of young people. It is best if children are taught something of substance in an illustrative way, but the point should not be lost in creative entertainment that only detracts from what is important. In his book *Peculiar Speech: Preaching to the Baptized,* William Willimon comments on how much ministry for children is easily trivialized and fails to meet youngsters' spiritual needs. He writes, "The Bible has the courage to discuss such concerns. Why can't we speak to children with as much depth and complexity as the Bible uses? With what sort of honesty would we have to speak of our family life if we spoke with the words of the Bible rather than with the language of sentimentality and trivialization?" (Grand Rapids, Mich.: Eerdmans, 1992, p. 55).

The responsibility of the children's sermon may be delegated to a youth worker, church leader or parent in the congregation, but I believe the pastor is the best person to give it. This helps children identify the pastor as a special teacher, a person to pay attention to and listen to. Admittedly, not all pastors are particularly gifted in interacting with or talking to children. In that case other spiritual leaders and people gifted in children's ministry should be encouraged to give the children's sermon. The pastor can provide oversight and information about the substance of the adult sermon and can lend authority to the person who teaches the children.

The children's sermon is also a good opportunity for children to pray out loud and in unison. Such a prayer is led by the adult and echoed by the children, and its content should relate to the children's sermon. This helps children learn how to pray out loud within the congregation. It also teaches them that prayer is a good way to respond to the Word of God when it is heard and understood.

Adults, in hearing the children's sermon, are helped by anticipating the focus of the sermon, possibly being introduced to the Scripture text and gaining a picture of what the exposition of God's Word may contain that morning.

Help children listen to "adult sermons" by encouraging them to listen when stories are being told. If your pastor rarely or never uses story illustrations, share this idea for helping you as a parent in the pew. Preachers want people to listen to what they have prepared, and most will be encouraged by your interest. There are magazines for pastors that contain sermon illustrations. Give your pastor a gift subscription. Also, huge volumes with nothing in them but illustrations and stories that help make a point are available for speakers, writers and preachers.

When the boys were quite young, I never worried too much if they fell asleep during the sermon. After all, in most schools kindergartners still take naps. And attention spans vary among children. But I wanted the boys to know that sermons were an important way to learn and be challenged by the Word of God. Reviewing the highlights after the service was one way I let them know the sermon was important.

I asked questions. "That was a good story today in the sermon. What did you learn about God in the story about the lighthouse?" As children get older, you can ask questions that will push them to listen for details. "That was a neat story about how the famous Mr. Moody came to believe in Jesus. What did the man who shared the gospel with Mr. Moody do for a living?" General questions can work with older youth who have become good listeners. "So, what did you learn from the sermon today?"

Turn about is fair play! Kids will ask parents questions, too, as they begin to really listen to sermons. Some kids will ask about the meaning of words. There will be phrases or expressions or intimations within a sermon that children will not grasp. Most of the time, children just let things beyond their understanding slip past. Sometimes they will whisper questions in the pew. Giving brief answers to some questions is appropriate; others need to be answered at a later time. Either way, be sure to respond respectfully to your children. If a question needs to be answered later, ask the child to remember the question and ask it again after church. If the question is truly important or interesting to children, they will not forget to ask. And they will actually listen to the information or answer you give them.

Some questions are answered as the sermon progresses. When you become aware that the child's question is being addressed from the pulpit, draw the child's attention to this. A quick whisper, with a nod of the head or a poke in the side, can tune a child in to the sermon just as his question is being answered. A great benefit to letting the sermon itself address questions is the way attention spans are lengthened. Children get the idea that to *keep listening* can be helpful.

Of course, not all sermons are put together or preached in a way that helps parents who are encouraging their children to pay attention. Again, making the most of the sermon after the service is often the only way. One parent shared with me that she let her kids draw a picture of what they heard in the sermon as it was being preached. It sounded like a good idea, but I hesitate to open the door to doodling and game-playing. Instead, I would suggest that the children draw pictures of what they learned *after* the service, and that the family discuss the sermon together.

Once I was talking about parenting in the pew with the father of a nine-year-old. He told me that he let his grade-schooler bring a "Find Waldo" book to church for the sermon time. He had simply never thought about asking his son to listen. He liked the idea of beginning with stories and illustrations. I encouraged my friend to leave Waldo at home and to work at helping his son find the joy of worship instead.

Some churches provide pads with puzzles and games and space to draw to keep children occupied during the "long parts" of worship. Not only is the use of these pads not confined to the "long parts," but it supports the idea that it is okay for kids to tune out during worship. The pads are provided to keep kids quiet, not to train them in worship. Using them may be easier, but the reward is paltry.

## Older Children and Sermons

After a "Parenting in the Pew" seminar, one teenager in our congregation "had" to sit with his parents again. This high-school sophomore joined his family as they all started over together in learning to worship. After a few weeks, I asked Chad whether he was still speaking to me and how he was doing.

Chad smiled easily and responded, "Oh, I like it. I never knew I could understand a sermon before. I don't mind at all."

I wish I had lots of stories like Chad's to tell you. Usually I don't get to visit a church other than the time I present "Parenting in the Pew," so most stories like Chad's are unknown to me.

But I have found that young people like to be challenged. Parents need to expect more from their children in church. Chad was asked to pay attention to a sermon; when he did, he discovered that there was meaning in it just for him.

The Atomic Praise Youth Choir made the same discovery. The choir had made significant progress in entering into the worship of God on Sundays. These junior-high and high-school kids were getting it. They paid attention and participated in readings, hymns, prayer and Scripture, and the music was increasingly directed toward God and not the congregation.

But when it came to sermon time, a sudden transformation took place. Alertness became lethargy, bright eyes became dull, and "teen slump" became the posture of choice. All this happened in the time it took for the Scripture reading to end and the pastor to pronounce the first word of his sermon. Why?

It was the lack of expectation. The kids had been tuning out habitually since childhood and had never been expected to listen. I couldn't poke all of them in the ribs, so I had to be creative. But not really all that creative; it didn't take much.

At choir practice, I shared my concern and expectation with them about the importance of listening to the sermon, the teaching from God's Word. After the "why," I suggested a training incentive. Every week at practice, I would ask three questions drawn from the sermon. I might ask about a detail in a story the pastor told, the text reference from which the sermon was drawn, a repeated phrase, or anything that might be gleaned by listening closely.

As the choir members got better at listening, my questions got harder. I might ask for the three-point outline that served as the framework of a sermon. The details became minute. It was really fun. If I forgot to quiz them, they would remind me! If I remembered wrong, I would be quickly corrected. One of the unanticipated benefits was how these young people began to anticipate questions I might ask.

I always tried to ask at least one question that centered on the sermon's main point. During the sermon, teenage heads would turn and look at me at strategic times to see whether I was writing a question for the next test. I wore a poker face. Sometimes as I asked the questions at practice, screams of joy erupted: "I knew it! I knew it! I knew you'd ask us that!"

All this teen attention didn't come, however, without an initial bribe. Any choir member who got all three questions perfectly correct (and I grade tough) got a piece of candy or a small item that was considered desirable for teens. They were not short of ideas for the rewards! After a short time, it was rare for anyone *not* to earn the reward unless they were not at worship. And worship attendance for some actually improved.

Tests such as those I gave the Atomic Praise can be given by any parent to older children and teens to help them learn to pay attention. The rewards can vary. If a family habitually goes out to eat after worship, the high scorer may pick the place. A special privilege or treat can be offered.

After a time, the reward will most likely be unnecessary. Learning to listen has its own reward. Chad and teens like him learn that they can understand a sermon and they won't mind at all.

### New Rules for a New Couch

Not all kids are as amiable as Chad. And I'm sure Chad's mom can testify that even he has had less-than-cooperative moments. It's not easy to change the rules with kids. It's not easy to enforce the rules, either. But parents do it all the time. We create new rules and make the effort to enforce them when an issue is important to us. So take heart if you didn't get an early start in training your children to worship.

Take a new couch or a new car. There were few rules for the old couch. You could lie on it any old way. You could drink grape juice and read the morning paper while sitting on its old cushions. An old car? Zip through the drive-thru for burgers and fries. Wipe up what you spill, no big deal. But a new couch? a new car? New rules.

No eating food on the new couch. Take your shoes off before putting your feet up. And the no-bouncing rule that was always in effect will now be enforced. And a new car? Forget the drive-thru for the first thousand miles.

Now kids may grumble and the whole family may need reminders, but everyone adjusts to consistent enforcement, and this means that the new car and couch stay new longer.

Your kids may grumble about worship-training. The whole family will have to work at commitment, but everyone will adjust, and the new way of going to church will soon become the best way of going to worship.

Sermons, the Lord's Prayer, doxologies and creeds are familiar parts of many services of worship. Doing old things with a new attitude gives refreshing life and deeper meaning to our habits of faith.

Young children learn the reasons behind ritual as they memorize the words. Older children confirm their identity in the family of God by sharing fully in the historical recitals that define what we believe. Teens learn that sermons contain old truth for today's world.

It is not easy for some families to do old things in a new way. A rebellious and disinterested teen needs honesty and encouragement. Parents need to give rewards for cooperation and express their appreciation, not just their expectations. "I want to let you know how thankful I am to have the whole family sitting together this Sunday. Worship with you means a whole lot to me"— such words can say a lot to a disgruntled teen. He or she may not let you know right away, but your appreciation is important.

New couches and new cars will be old someday. But not our relationship with God. Scripture tells us that God's faithfulness never fails, and his mercies are new every morning. Our children will be old someday. But new rules can help them hear the faithfulness and mercy of God that last forever.

# Saving Up
# for Something
# Special

# 9

**P**G" and "PG-13" are signals in our moviegoing culture that parents need to be involved in selecting entertainment for children. Parental guidance provides necessary oversight and wisdom in many decisions that directly affect children. As the significance of a decision increases, the guidance given by parents becomes more important accordingly.

A teenager's visit to a used-car lot needs to be a PG experience. Toddlers' viewing of Saturday-morning cartoons needs to be a PG experience. Invitations to sleep over (these used to be called slumber parties) for grade-schoolers need to be PG

experiences. Parental guidance is needed for car-buying, TV-
watching and friend-selecting. Parenting in the pew, training
children to worship, is a marathon PG experience too. And it
is never more important than when it concerns the sacraments
of the church.

Denominational theology and congregational tradition will
determine, to a significant degree, the timing and style of sacramental participation. I don't intend to discuss denominational
distinctions that are argued and defended by brother and sister
Christians around the world. But I *will* argue that it's very
important that children recognize the extra-special significance
of the biblical expressions of belief exemplified in the sacraments.

The sacraments of the faith are extra-special expressions of
what we believe. Regardless of denominational distinctions, the
sacraments are serious. Whether one holds to symbol or to
substance, the sacredness of sacraments needs to be communicated to children.

Scraps of red, white and blue fabric are not special until they
are sewn together to become the national flag. As the flag, it is
protected by law and regulations for its use and care. A flag is
no longer just red, white and blue fabric. Once made into a flag,
the red, white and blue fabric is not appropriately used as a
tablecloth or a bedspread.

Sacraments are symbols: water, bread, juice or wine. But they
are not *just* symbols. They have been made sacred and special
for use in the church to help us remember and rehearse the
salvation of God. The sacred nature of these common elements
in the ritual of the church comes from the Word of God that
once more chooses to be made visible among us "full of grace

and truth" (John 1:14). We need to help our children handle these elements with reverent care.

## Baptism

Baptism is a symbol of cleansing and inclusion. The need to be cleansed from sin and initiated into the family of God is based on doctrinal tenets of Jewish-Christian heritage. Infant baptism, depending on the denomination, symbolizes either the promise or the actuality of those tenets.

As parents, we must take our vows at the time of an infant's baptism with utmost integrity. These vows may be taken on behalf of the infant in faith, or we may be promising to train the child in the faith. Talking with the pastor about the meaning of infant baptism in the denominational or congregational tradition of the family can be very helpful to parents who wish to understand and honor baptismal commitments.

In any case, as the child grows older she will begin to see the baptism of others in the congregation. Parents can use these occasions to teach children the significance of their own baptism. Most children are curious about how they looked or what they did as infants. They like to hear stories about themselves in a time that they cannot remember. Baptism can be a profound reminder to a child about who they are in the family of God.

When adults or children are baptized in a congregation, parents can help their children understand the significance of the event. If the children were baptized as infants, they can be reminded of "the day this happened to you." After worship, baptismal clothing can be brought out and pictures of the event shown to the child. The story of the day they were baptized can be told and retold. This in itself is an ancient tradition of our faith.

> Hear, O Israel: The LORD our God, the LORD is one. Love the LORD your God with all your heart and with all your soul and with all your strength. These commandments that I give you today are to be upon your hearts. Impress them on your children. Talk about them when you sit at home and when you walk along the road, when you lie down and when you get up. (Deuteronomy 6:4-7)

Commandments, history and the stories of redemption were all meant to be told and retold from generation to generation in the family of God. Sacramental rituals in the church can be the generational bonds that help children relate to the truths of God they need to embrace within the body of Christ.

One definition of a sacrament is "a visible sign of invisible Grace." Talking about the meaning of the baptismal sacrament can help children gain a picture of God's love and provision of care and acceptance for his children.

Adult baptism is often an adolescent experience. Teens want to be accepted by the church and by God. The turbulence of the teenage years prompts many to seek repentance and the chance to "start over." So help your older children think through what it means to be baptized. You can facilitate discussions with the pastor and make sure your son or daughter can attend instruction sessions for the sacrament. Help foster an appropriate sense of seriousness concerning the decision. Teenagers are easily distracted by many things. Cars, clothes, the opposite sex, sports and schoolwork vie for priority consideration in the daily life of a teen. But you can help your teen keep priorities straight, modify schedules and put first things first.

As a parent, you can *help*. But you can't *do* the right things for your adolescent child.

Adult baptism is a decision that must be made by the individual, in submission to the authority of the church, and with the oversight of the pastor and elders. You need to help your teen think through the motivation for his desire to be baptized. Make sure he understands that baptism is *not* something done automatically at a certain age. Try to discern whether your adolescent is seeking baptism because of peer pressure or the expectations of others.

### The Lord's Supper

Jesus instituted the sacrament of Communion to help us remember the sacrifice that allowed us to be reconciled to God. It is an intimate expression of our need for God's life to be our life. Doctrinally and historically, it is the most significant confession of Christ Jesus as Lord and Savior. As the Lord's Supper was instituted in a community of believers, it also helps us become more aware of our unity in the body of Christ.

The Gospels of Matthew, Mark and Luke tell of the last meal Jesus ate with his disciples on the night of his arrest. Jesus took the symbols of the Passover meal and used them to explain a redemption that was even greater than that which saved Hebrew believers from death before their exodus from Egypt. The apostle Paul summarizes the institution of the sacred meal this way:

For I received from the Lord what I also passed on to you. The Lord Jesus, on the night he was betrayed, took bread, and when he had given thanks, he broke it and said, "This is my body, which is for you; do this in remembrance of me." In the same way, after supper he took the cup, saying, "This cup is the new covenant in my blood; do this, whenever you drink it, in remembrance of me." For whenever you eat this bread and drink this cup, you proclaim the Lord's death until he comes. (1 Corinthians 11:23-26)

Paul continues in this passage to explain the serious nature of this sacrament of remembrance. He warns against eating the bread or drinking the cup of the Lord in "an unworthy manner," and says that those who commune must "examine" themselves before they eat the bread and drink the cup. (See verses 27-30.)

With this admonition in mind, taking the Lord's Supper is a serious celebration of God's goodness and grace. The Scriptures encourage Christians to approach the table of the Lord with earnest self-examination, confession and a humble and grateful heart.

This is certainly an area of parenting in the pew that requires parents' wisdom and oversight of their children. Not all parents will agree with my strategy for training children regarding the Lord's Supper. But I hope that this discussion will encourage parents to be very careful and thoughtful in how they help their children prepare for this sacrament of the church.

## Anticipation

The fact that a young person can explain where babies come from doesn't mean that she is ready to become a parent. Explaining the mechanical "how-to's" of sex does not qualify a person for the responsibilities of an intimate relationship. Time, training and testing are needed before one is prepared for sexual responsibility.

The sacramental responsibility of partaking of the Lord's

Supper, as laid out in Scripture, is just as serious. Young children may be able to recite John 3:16 and believe it with all their hearts, but this doesn't mean they are necessarily ready for the responsibility and self-examination that comes with this sacramental expression of faith.

Anticipation is the best preparation for appreciation. It is good for children to wait for what is truly important. In American culture, fifteen-year-olds count down the days for the automotive rite of passage. Advent calendars help children wait and watch for Christmas. Christian parents teach their children that waiting until marriage for sex can provide the security needed for its full enjoyment and fulfillment.

Some faith communities give grapes or "little sips" to children during Communion so they do not feel left out. I think this is unwise. Every day, parents deny their children experiences that are beyond a child's capacity to appreciate or handle well. A six-year-old does not get to drive a car just because his sixteen-year-old sister can. A three-year-old does not go to kindergarten with her five-year-old sibling, no matter how badly she fusses about being left out. The sacred must be treated with at least the same amount of care and oversight for the welfare of the child.

It is traditional in some churches to allow even very young children to take Communion. Although it is certainly possible to help children grow to appreciate what is already theirs, it is difficult. Familiarity may not breed contempt in this situation, but it certainly can dull an appreciation for what should be special.

We Christian parents need to help our children anticipate the joys of participating in the supper of the Lord. The guideline for our home was this: When Robert and Scott were able to give their own testimony of faith before the congregation, they were old enough to be responsible to participate in Communion with God's people. It seemed reasonable to us that when a young person was able to share clearly with others *in his own words* what he believed, he was old enough to share in the meal the Lord gave to his community of believers.

When our children were quite young, they could explain the basic elements of the gospel. They had genuine experiences of salvation when they asked Jesus to forgive their rebellion and enter their lives. Our children had an assurance of God's presence in their lives through some painful experiences. At an early age they began asking to take Communion. They longed to participate.

Our response was always the same: "Are you ready to write out what you believe about Jesus, and give this testimony to the church family during worship?" When they were very young the answer to both questions was "No, not yet" or "Do I have to?" As they grew older, they would say yes to the first question about writing out their testimony. But it was still "I can't" or "Do I have to?" to the second. It was intimidating for them to think about speaking alone in front of the whole church. For us, this was a valid sign that they were still not quite mature or prepared enough to partake of the Communion elements with the congregation either.

Finally, Robert and Scott were able to say yes to both questions with a measure of confidence and maturity that indicated they were in fact ready to stand on their own in the community of God's people.

**Preparation**
What a joy it was to read what they wrote about their faith! And

it was a blessing to hear their confession of faith spoken from their hearts before the Lord and his people in worship. It was not that they had reached a certain chronological age, but that they had attained a level of spiritual and social maturity. Participation in the Lord's Supper requires both these dimensions.

A young person should enter into Communion with God's people on his own two feet. We did not write our children's testimonies. Robert and Scott did not memorize and recite anything that had been written by others.

Communicant classes determined by age alone do not necessarily measure individual faith, understanding or even social maturity. Innocent, enthusiastic desire is not a proper indicator of spiritual readiness for entering into Holy Communion.

The indicators we used were commitment, cost, personal initiative and follow-through. Given the personalities and opportunities of other families' worship situations and practices, as well as particulars in denominational theology, you may choose different indicators as you prepare your children for this sacred experience.

Think this through with your family, study the significance of Communion in your faith tradition, talk to your pastor and help your children share in this covenant with great seriousness. Setting this table for us cost God the life of his only Son.

If your children feel left out, neglected or deprived because they can't participate in the sacrament, it may be because explanations have been given in terms of denial, not anticipation. "No, you can't" is very different from "Not yet; it's important to wait." Parents should communicate a longing for their children to participate: "Oh, I can hardly wait until you're old enough!"

Delay is not denial. Waiting for the proper time is not idle waiting, nor is it empty. Anticipation is the best preparation for the proper moment of fulfillment.

## Practice

Because the price of this sacred meal is so high, children need to begin yearning for its taste at an early age. Whether Communion elements are given in the pew or at the front of the sanctuary in your church, your children can share the experience vicariously by just being with you.

As we sat in the pew, or when we knelt at a prayer rail, I would hold the bread and cup in my hands. I had each of the boys cup his hands around mine. With each element I would whisper the mystery of meaning in these sacred symbols as we contemplated them together. Then I took in the elements of bread and cup. Immediately, I would again hold their hands and tell them that God's love was extended to them in a special way in Christ's death and resurrection. They were drawn into the remembrance with me.

When the boys were toddlers, my explanation sounded something like this: "This is to remind us of how Jesus had to be hurt and broken to forgive us for all we do wrong." Or I would remind them of a time during the week when they had been hurt. "Do you remember when you cut your finger this week? It hurt a lot, huh? It hurt Jesus way more than that when he died on the cross for us." Always it was a time to do what Jesus commanded when he instituted the supper. "Wow, God sure does love us. We need to be very thankful that Jesus gave his life for us."

In Communion we celebrate the final words of Jesus' institution of the sacrament: "I tell you, I will not drink of this fruit of the vine from now on until that day when I drink it anew with you in my Father's kingdom" (Matthew 26:29). The celebration of salvation from sin is a celebration of being saved for our heavenly home. Jesus is not dead, but alive. He has gone ahead of us to prepare a place for us. The Communion table is a table of preparation for a coming banquet of joy and fulfillment.

Children love parties, and this sacrament is a reminder that our God is a God of joy and celebration. And someday we will celebrate with God the victory over death and sin and lostness won for us by "the Lamb who was slain."

I am sure that my toddlers did not understand all of this truth on a theological level, but during Communion after Communion for many years they grew into the mystery. They knew by my tears, the gravity of my voice and the persistence of the message that this was a profoundly significant event. They knew by my joy in being set free to start over that Communion was a celebration of being loved by God.

As the boys grew up, explanations deepened. "To think of how much God loved us . . . how much it cost Jesus to be obedient unto death just to save us . . . what it must have meant for God to take our sin and place it on his perfect Son . . ."

Little by little the message, the elements, the symbolism and the implications for the boys' own faith took root. As they grew older, I began to see an increasingly serious mood and manner in them during the service of the sacrament. They would touch the elements reverently, and their sense of awe for this ultimate gift would be evident. Joy deepened; resting in God's secure love brought great peace.

Today when we take Communion together, one dear son on

each side of me, all we say is "This is Christ's body, broken for you," and then "This is the blood of Christ, shed for you." We know what we mean. We know what Christ meant.

It has been well worth the wait. When I look at Robert and Scott, who are now both taller than I am, I know this is not a sacrifice they take for granted.

## Setting an Example

The boys have also been very aware of the times when I have not been able to partake of the Lord's Supper. They know when I have examined my heart and found things not right with God. They know about the time of pain after the murder of a dear friend. I was hurt and angry and needed to sort things out with God first. They know about the time I was wrestling with resentment after a difficult time with my husband—their father and our pastor.

In these situations, I had to remind the boys of Paul's admonition not to take Communion unworthily. I had to refrain until I could work things through in prayer with the Lord. And my children saw that God's grace was always sufficient to restore me through Scripture, prayer, repentance, confession and reconciliation. My children have seen what it means to take sin seriously. They have also seen what it means to take the grace of God seriously.

The redemption offered by Christ in his death and remembered at Communion cannot be taken lightly. When Rob and Scott saw that I could return to the holy table forgiven and full of joy, they learned that they could too. When my sons sensed my anticipation of the heavenly banquet in the kingdom of God, they began to long for this celebration too.

Turn your eyes upon Jesus;
Look full in his wonderful face,
And the things of earth will grow strangely dim
In the light of his glory and grace. (Helen Lemmel, 1922)
There are many things in life worth waiting for. I look forward
to the day I drink "this fruit of the vine" in the kingdom of my
Savior. And I am grateful that my children look forward to the
same party, and that we get to begin the celebration now.

# The
# Holy
# Hug

# 10

**P**eople often choose churches in the same way they pick
dry cleaners. Do they do it the way I like it? Is there
just enough starch to make it crisp, but not uncomfort-
able? Are the creases straight? Do they spot-clean well? Do they
do alterations? Are they conveniently located and reasonable in
cost?

Church selection is a matter of personal preference. The decision is often based on how a congregation matches up with
what one likes. Music, sermon length, preaching style, congregational demographics, sanctuary decor, dress code, denomina-

tion and the greeters' degree of friendliness are factors in the church-shopping enterprise.

People attend church to feel better, please parents, maintain a healthy habit, set a good example, fulfill a role, get help with a problem, learn about the Bible, pray with others, teach children values, keep kids busy, and to be baptized, married and buried.

But all this is not enough for a lifetime of faith. All of the things that attract you can change. Churches and dry cleaners can go through management overhauls that make you wonder why you ever went there in the first place.

Only God, revealed in Jesus Christ, is "the same yesterday and today and forever" (Hebrews 13:8). Only in God can we find hope. Only when we learn to worship, rather than just going to church, will we be at rest. Only God offers stability in our rapidly changing and decaying world.

Worship is a gem of truth in a marketplace of cheap imitations. Encountering God is meeting the Reality that undergirds all of life. When you introduce your children to what is completely genuine, you are equipping them to judge all the other experiences and possibilities that will come to them.

Many young people today wonder whether there is anything certain, anyone they can completely trust. Traditions, whether family, country or faith, are not automatically embraced. Our children are growing up in a time when religious hypocrisy is declining. Fewer people are "just-Christmas-and-Easter" nominal Christians. In many respects evil is more openly evil. People are less embarrassed by lapses in common morality. Fewer young people will continue in church out of habit or family tradition.

Great numbers of young people are growing up in the spiritual vacuum created by the exclusion of God from home and society. People are increasingly wary of being manipulated by those who popularly franchise religious experience. The only One who can completely fill the spiritual vacuum is God revealed in Jesus Christ. And like Augustine's heart sixteen centuries ago, the hearts of our children are restless.

The sabbath rest of God still remains for those who enter into God's presence and receive his mercy and grace to help in times of need (Hebrews 4:9-16). Worship teaches us how to enter into the sabbath rest—to cease striving and to know our God (Psalm 46:10).

Children need to rest these days. Even so, much of their recreation is competition, strife and performance. Few children are "re-created" by sports. Winning gives the only momentary joy. Losing, failing, coming in second rob many children of any enjoyment in even the effort.

Parents, too, need to rest these days. The Gospel of Jesus Christ gives us the freedom to fail. The Lord of life has come to call not the righteous but sinners to repentance. This is very good news to me. I rejoice that Jesus loves me. I can be honest with him about the difficulties, disappointments and sin in my life. He will not turn away.

Parenting is much harder than I thought it would be. And parenting in the pew may be the hardest parenting of all. I have failed more than I thought I ever would. I have done some really stupid things as a mother, even at worship. I have felt things that I didn't think real mothers could feel about their offspring. But always I could go to Jesus. Always his mercy was new every morning. His faithfulness is indeed great.

And I could go to the boys. I could own up to my lack of wisdom, my shortcomings, my failure. And, just as with the Lord, it was no surprise to them. My children have forgiven me many times.

This capacity to weather the storms of child-rearing came in significant measure because of our "oasis" of rest and reminder. The pew has been a place of love for us. We have rested with each other. I think we could rest like this because we were aware of being in the presence of a perfect Parent. Our Father was watching over us.

Worship has been a time of remembrance to us because our Father meets us there and tells us the way back home. Over and over again God meets us and reminds us of his love and mercy. We have been reminded Sunday after Sunday that he knows it all and loves us still.

Through worshiping together, my children and I have become friends before the throne of grace. As fellow sinners, we worship our Father who forgives. In worship we have learned to love God and accept his mercy. In worship we have learned to love each other and accept our failures.

God must be real in our experience of faith. He must be known and encountered. We cannot be satisfied with worship that simply fulfills social and religious obligations. God must be heard. We need to teach our children what it means to touch the hem of his garment and be healed. Our children need to clamber into the loving lap of the Savior. He yearns for the companionship of children and longs to bless them.

Let the little children come to me, and do not hinder them,

for the kingdom of God belongs to such as these. (Mark 10:14) Parenting in the pew is a response to Jesus' admonition not to

hinder our children. It is one way to take our children by the
hand and guide them to the embrace and blessing of the Savior.
Teaching your children to worship is helping them learn to give
the Lord a holy hug—to bless him with the embrace of their
souls.

I remember how, when the boys were quite small, they would
bring me their "writing"—jagged scribbles on scraps of paper—
and I would display it on the refrigerator. And it occurs to me
that worship is a time when I bring the scribbles of my life and
my Father takes them and puts them all on his heavenly refrigerator—all the scribbles, not just the pretty ones or the ones that
make sense. He is the perfect Parent who always sees what's
really there. This is the Father of truth and grace I wanted my
children to know and love.

Today I watch my sons, almost men, bring their scribbles—
the struggles and joys of their life with God—to worship. And
as I see their scribbles placed on our Father's refrigerator, I see
my sons more clearly in the pew. Sitting beside me is the han-
diwork of God. In the presence of our Father, my sons have
become my brothers. There is no greater joy for any parent in
the pew.